New Dimensions
in Healing

New Dimensions in Healing

H-A

channelled
through the mediumship of

Tony Neate

The Eye of Gaza Press

New Dimensions in Healing

This edition was first published in Great Britain   2007

Copyright © 1999, 2007   Tony Neate

Cover design & artwork © 2007 Tony Roeber

IBSN number 1 873545 04 5

Edited by Ann Neate & Greg Branson

The author of this book is not a physician, and the ideas, procedures and suggestions in this book are not intended to replace the medical and legal advice of trained professionals. All matters regarding your health require medical supervision. Consult your medical practitioner about any condition that may require diagnosis or treatment.

Published by the Eye of Gaza Press,
BCM - New Age, London, WC1N 3XX   (0207 713 7159)
Printed by Carlyon Print

Contents

TONY NEATE FCOH, MNFSH

Tony Neate is a well-known and respected channeller of H-A. He has brought through this wisdom from the higher levels of consciousness since the 1950's. The teachings have been published in a number of books, including *The Guide Book* and *H-A on Life and Living.*

Tony co-founded the Atlantean Society in 1957 with Murry Hope and, in the 1970's, he started a health food business with his wife, Ann. In 1975, he became interested in the complementary treatment of cancer when his mother died of stomach cancer. He had the good fortune to tour Europe with Dr Alec Forbes, a retired consultant physician and first medical director of the Bristol Cancer Help Centre, visiting Dr Hans Moolenburgh in Holland and Dr Hans Nieper in Germany, both specialists in the field.

In 1979, he co-founded the Nature's Own/Cytoplan group which produce nutritional supplements to the highest ethical standards. In the early 1980's, Tony directed a Cancer Help Centre in Cheltenham with his wife, Ann, and Dr John Cosh and later became Chair of the Holistic Council for Cancer. He succeeded the late Sir George Trevelyan as Chair of WrekinTrust, and for 6 years was also Chair of the Council of a Rudolf Steiner School.

In 1981, Tony co-founded the Runnings Park Centre for Health, Healing and Self-Development in Malvern, which ran for 21 years, and also the College of Healing which provides a highly accredited Healing Course. He also co-founded the Confederation of Healing Organisations.

In 1990, Tony started the School of Channelling, and is now its Patron. He is the author of *Channelling for Everyone,* published in 1997 by Piatkus. It has also been published in the USA, Germany and Bulgaria.

Currently, he is Chair of the Spirit Release Foundation, an organisation founded in 1999 by a small group of medical and complementary practitioners who felt there was a need for a new open approach to spirit release, combining the intuitive and inter-active approaches.

Who is H-A?

H-A is a being from the higher planes of consciousness who was first channelled by Tony Neate in 1956. Tony was already practising as a trance medium with a group of friends who were told to expect 'a great teacher.' A few weeks later, Tony tuned into H-A.

"Above all it was the aura and the light that he emanated that I was aware of; a feeling of immense energy and power and light, yet a *complete* humility." That was Tony's first impression and today he still experiences H-A in this way.

When asked "Who are you?", he replied: "I am what I am, no more, no less. I am part of the universal divinity, as you are part of the universal divinity…I have come from beyond the confines of Earth to help the planet in its present stage of evolution…." When questioned further, he said he had had an incarnation as a high priest in Atlantis, named Helio-Arcanophus, which means 'High Priest of the Sun'. He gives an understanding which supports humanity and Planet Earth as we move from the Piscean Age into the Aquarian Age. It is a teaching of unconditional love, forgiveness and respect.

This much needed teaching encourages us to move beyond negative thought patterns such as jealousy and revenge, judgement and blame, into a new consciousness of spiritual self-responsibility, respect for self and others, empowerment and unconditional love - acknowledging the divinity within each unique individual soul. H-A has also taught us new healing concepts which have provided an enlightened understanding of how we can help one another on our evolutionary journey.

H-A's wisdom and philosophy is accessible to all and is now channelled through other mediums.

ACKNOWLEDGMENTS

I would like to thank Helen Lees and Jo Morgan for the hours of work they put into compiling the original collection of these teachings, from the many lectures given by H-A in 1999.

Thanks must also go to Gilly Wilmot who channelled much of the chapter on Basic Karmic Healing.   Ann Neate

Chapter 1

THE NEW HEALING MODALITIES

Dear Healer, these new modalities are being offered to you in the spirit of unconditional love, beyond judgment and manipulation. They are given as a resource to stimulate and give birth to new ideas and new approaches within you, to help you find your own level of self-empowerment and self-realisation, and for you to help others to do likewise.

These modalities, with your assistance, will enable a patient to deal with unreleased levels of stuckness which the more general forms of healing will not reach. They provide a new look at the energy healing process and offer an exciting extension to your healing, which includes methods of focusing healing energy in a more detailed and subtle way, to meet specific needs. It includes the understanding that a healer channels cosmic divine energy, an energy that is in the universe for anyone to harness.

As you, the healer, harness that energy, you allow your mind and body to be used to transform it into a frequency that is suitable for your client. The energy reaches the client and merges with their subtle energies, touching them on the most sensitive, the finest level of their being and from that level it filters through to other levels of consciousness that make up that person as a whole being.

When a person becomes dis-eased, it means that those different levels of consciousness, the mind, the emotions, the physical and the spirit that make up that person as a whole being, have become out of balance. They no longer resonate harmoniously; they are like musical notes jarring with each other. This is because the state of the person's whole being reflects the way they are, their under-standing, and how they are dealing with their life at that time. Any one moment in time reflects all that a person has ever been in this

1

and past lives, both in and out of the body and before human experience – it is a synchronicity of all their accumulated experience.

Spirit and Soul

Your spirit is made up of two aspects that are connected: one, the Higher Self, does not actually incarnate; and the other, the soul aspect, incarnates and merges into your physical mind, your brain and your body. This is the part that experiences life in the now, returning at the death of the body to the spirit, adding to its overall sum total of experience. Your Higher Self is the wisdom that flows from your spirit, connecting with the finer levels of your soul and the stronger the connection, the more inspiration you will receive in directing your physical life.

It is the way in which all these levels come together that allows you to prepare for handling your life, and to develop the ability to accept and deal with the challenges that will face you.

Karmic Healing

The healing that you have used until now and that most healers on your planet use is what I call Karmic Healing. This focuses on healing the soul in relation to the body. You channel cosmic energy to your client, allowing that energy to circulate within their being, releasing stiffness of energy, stiffness of thought, helping them to connect with their Higher Self.

This may bring forward within a person the question as to what might have contributed to their illness and what they would like to do about it. It can enable your client to discover something for themselves from the deepest part of their being, that part which connects with their karmic path, their *raison d'etre* in this life, and to make a choice. If on a very deep level there is a commitment on their part to becoming whole, the healing may seem to be miraculous and will enlighten their understanding.

> *Remember, in giving healing to another you are not putting anything right. You are enabling them to move beyond the need of their particular problem.*

Advanced Energy Healing

This is a specialised Karmic Healing on a finer spiritual level. The healer is not only channelling the energy that they normally channel to give healing but they are also contacting energy on a more potent level to enhance what they are doing. I introduce this because I feel the planet is ready to understand healing in a more subtle way. I see healing not as curing, but as enabling a person to find their right level of being and, therefore, able to be in charge of their own life.

On this planet at the moment there is a great deal of pollution at all levels, physical, climatic, planetary and spiritual, and so it is important for people to appreciate how to deal with different levels of disharmony. If, for example, they feel and/or the healer senses that there is an energy around them that is having a detrimental effect – perhaps there is a form of attachment which something within the person has drawn towards themselves – then they need a more advanced form of healing to deal with this, which also means the healer contacting a higher level of consciousness.

Conceptional Healing

This next healing modality is what I call Conceptional Healing. When a spirit enters at the moment of conception, it has been drawn towards its parents because the needs of all three have coincided. First of all it has to face entry into the body at the moment of fertilisation. That spirit may be on its own, or there may be another spirit also drawn towards that fertilised seed. This moment of choosing who comes in can be quite traumatic in itself. Once it is in the embryo, the spirit is very much in the process of merging with the energy of the mother and the energy transferred from the father. This in itself is one of the most significant moments in the life of any spirit, fusing with the physical embryo, so much is dependent upon it and it is dependent on so much. This is why I have introduced Conceptional Healing, a process which needs to be facilitated by a healer.

Ancestral Healing

However, there may be deeper or more complex reasons for the imbalance. There is the question of the parents and the genetic

DNA energy which they have inherited physically from their parents and so forth, back through their antecedents, and how this blends with the karma of their spirit. This is where I have introduced Ancestral Healing. This again is best facilitated by a healer/therapist.

Homoeopathic Healing

Then looking at your world, your solar system and this part of the universe, I have been very conscious of the intensification of cosmic energies around this planet, partly due to the eclipse in summer 1999, partly due to the line up of planets in June 2000 and very much to do with the transition from one great Solar Age to the next, reaching a climax in 2012. *

The energies around the planet have really 'hotted up' and Earth is facing a cathartic crisis in finding the balance between light and shadow on all levels. At any one moment it could soar in either direction, whereas what it needs above all is to maintain a balance. That balance has to be found through gentleness, through subtlety, through sensitivity, and therefore there are occasions when one will need to resort to what I call Homoeopathic Healing. It is a form of healing that is particularly effective with people who are very aware or very sensitive psychically, for it uses a very fine, delicate energy that goes right to the Higher Self aspect of the spirit.

Homeopathic healing can be offered to a single person or to a single spirit trapped within an unresolved trauma, or rigid archetypal situation. It can also be used in conjunction with other healing modalities. This modality is a new way of applying healing to your client, or to a traumatised spirit.

Archetypal Healing

Then there is another dimension to a spirit's karma, and that is the energy that it carries from the group soul with which it has been connected. These group situations can reflect religious beliefs, political beliefs, and collective beliefs of any kind. Immediately a group of people come together and form some sort of society, it carries with it the collective archetypal energy of that society, its customs, etc. This can become a burden, even a chain from the past, especially when there have been many incarnations into the same archetypal group. For this type of situation I have introduced Archetypal Healing, for yourself, your group or to guide another.

Planetary Healing

I describe this healing modality as Planetary Healing because it acknowledges the other modalities, incorporating them into one healing session in order to deal with issues having a wider significance. This would be especially appropriate for a troubled community, country or continent, and needs to be given by a group.

Peace Healing

Finally, when there is conflict between two people or two opposing factions or between countries, and this has gone on for a long time, to break up the entrenched attitudes in order to bring in the necessary harmony, a higher/more refined form of planetary healing is required. I have called this 'Peace Healing.'

OVERVIEW

The days of just giving healing to someone – the healer bringing the 'God energy to make you whole' – are past. That was of the Piscean Age. This coming Age of Aquarius we are entering is an age of self-responsibility, self-realisation and self-empowerment. The types of healing that I am trying to steer you into are more appropriate to the Aquarian Age, as they are bringing to the surface the opportunity for the patient to make their own decisions and to take responsibility for their health on every level.

That is perhaps the most fundamental difference between the approach to healing that I am offering and earlier concepts of healing, sometimes called spiritual healing, faith healing and so forth, where the attitude towards the healing has been authoritarian and 'a higher power puts you right' just as when you go to the doctor. We are moving out of that ethos into a new one, and those who are not prepared to follow this new ethos will in time find it very difficult. But of course it is their choice.

In my opinion, these new modalities provide approaches to healing that will enable you to reach out and find levels of support for your clients, which hitherto you have been unable to achieve.

When you realise that the normal Karmic Healing you are giving is not actually producing a response, and that it requires something more specific in order to help your client forward, this is the moment when you could consider using one or more of these healing modalities. I have always encouraged healers to understand their client on a psychological level, so that if emotional issues are raised, it will indicate to you the form of modality to use.

These healing modalities do not necessarily result in miracles, for miracles lie with the patient, not the healer. However, they will enable the patient to deal with unreleased levels of inner stuckness that the more general form of Karmic Healing will not reach.

The time has come to take healing forward into a new dimension and to develop your individual healing potential. These are guidelines that will enable you to take that step.

* "The Sun passes slowly on its majestic march through the Zodiac, on a clockwise course, taking rather over 2,000 years to cross one of the signs. The measure is taken from the position of the Sun at the Vernal Equinox on March 21st. This movement is known as the Precession of the Equinoxes. It takes 25,920 years for it to pass through the entire Zodiac, and this is known as the Cosmic Day. The Sun is now moving from Pisces into Aquarius, and we speak therefore of the entry into the Aquarian Age. For the previous 2,000 years it was in Pisces and before that in the Ram (Aries), having passed out of the Bull (Taurus)."

Extract from *Twelve Seats at the Round Table* by Sir George Trevelyan.

Chapter 2

SPIRIT AND ITS
DIRECTIONAL IMPULSE

The challenges for a spirit, both before and after incarnating, the problems it encounters and its spiritual makeup on all levels, are all part of its directional impulse, and healing can play an important role in helping it on its journey. Remember that the wisdom of your spirit determines how you live your life.

The Spirit incarnates
The spirit is an energy force. When it leaves the Godhead as a lone creative thought with free will and choice, it has within it a unique 'directional impulse' that needs to expand and find expression. It does not come into physical incarnation at this point but goes through a whole level of pre-human existence in which the needs of its 'directional impulse' begin to develop. So, when it does incarnate, it brings with it an impulse that has already started to build.

On one level it has nothing, neither experience nor understanding to draw upon, but a blank page on which to start writing its journal. In another sense, it comes with everything for it is a part of God; and it is important to understand that. It goes through various processes of learning and it has the opportunity of creating its own vision, its own mission and its own direction.

Most spirits choose some form of physical incarnation, either on planet Earth or on some other planet or star in the universe – and let me add that there is more than one universe. Your spirit has chosen this particular universe in which to experience. It needs to spend some time coming to terms with what it is, why it is, where it is, and how, why and where it needs to direct itself.

Incarnating into a physical body gives a spirit an opportunity to experience feelings and visions physically, to ground love through the emotions into physical living, experiencing how the emotions affect the physical body. It can also learn that an understanding and awareness between spirit and physical life can enable it to find true harmony and fulfilment as a whole being. Karmic Healing and the subsequent integration can help this awareness.

Light and Shadow
One of the very early lessons that a spirit must face is that having choice means it has to understand the difference between light and shadow or, as you may refer to it in a more orthodox way, good and bad, heaven and hell. I prefer light and shadow, although heaven and hell are terms which humans use. *They represent the two extremes, the two extreme possibilities of your choice.*

You have decided to embark on physical experience in *homo sapiens* on Earth. Now, you are helped and guided by other spirits to make your first choice into a physical body and you enter at the moment of conception.

When you come into incarnation you have the unconscious memory of the freedom of being in spirit, unconstrained by the small vehicle you inhabit, this vehicle of the flesh that enables you to experience physically. You have the memory of that freedom of movement through space, beyond linear time, to go where you will, to experience and to grow in wisdom. You bring that memory unconsciously into your Earth experience, because you are here to gain wisdom through absorbing information and knowledge through physical life to a high level of understanding, for wisdom is a state of deeply understanding the relationship to life itself. It is a fundamental energy of creativity.

Encountering Humanness
You are born with an unconscious awareness of all that you have been and known. This is imprinted into the very cellular structure of your body. All of your body knows what you have been and where you have been. As well as the body, you have emotions, you have a mind, and you have a very large spirit. You also have a personality that is there to make sure that you stay focused on the physical plane. You enter into a particular energy of time when you incarnate and it is as though you have an agreement that you will do what you have to do in so many years; and your personality

8

helps you to focus on your particular task of learning. It is physicalised and that is good because it is grounding you, it is keeping you here to see what is going on within Earth experience, for that is where your learning lies.

That first incarnation is a tremendous challenge, for you are truly in a world of the unknown, encountering experiences that you have never encountered before, experiences that may have been shown to you but until you actually experience them for yourself they are just an idea, a concept.

Establishing the Soul

The soul aspect of your spirit, the aspect that incarnates, needs to understand density, gravity and time. But because it seeks to be so close to Earth, it forgets, unless it is constantly in touch with its higher spirit aspect, that the pains of life are chosen; and that the pain, in fact, does not have to be pain once it is accepted as experience chosen for growth. It is perceived as pain by the personality and so there can be an avoidance of the body and a desire to go out to the spirit.

Unfortunately, you then have a problem both ways. You cannot really do what you came to do because the pain tends to create stuckness. You do not want any more pain, but on the other hand, you do not want to take risks even if they help you to grow. For the deeper you go into your being, the more problems and painful experiences you will find stored deep down in your being. There is a temptation to disappear out of the flesh, out of those emotions, out into the cosmos where you were once so free.

THE SUBTLE BODIES, CHAKRAS AND AURIC FIELD

The subtle bodies represent layers of consciousness between the spirit and the physical body. The spirit has two aspects: the Higher Self, which contains your spiritual karma, the sum total of everything you have experienced in or out of the physical body; the other aspect is what I would term your 'soul'. This is the aspect of you that is present in your physical body, providing the link between your Higher Self and all the different layers of consciousness. These layers are what I call 'subtle bodies', through which your soul communicates to connect with the physical body, which includes the physical brain.

9

The nearest subtle body to the physical is the 'etheric' which is the same shape as your physical body. After that, the subtle bodies become like bubbles of energy, getting subtler and subtler, until they become in contact with the soul.

Between each subtle body there is a vortex of energy called a 'chakra', which is like a spinning wheel of energy connecting one subtle body with the next. An important part of the healing process is to ensure that the major chakras and the subtle bodies are balanced so that there is a unity of energy between the soul and the physical body. The challenge of experiencing in the physical body is to bring the understanding of your Higher Self, through your soul aspect to your conscious mind and thence to your whole being.

Now, if one of those chakras becomes out of balance which can happen if a person is out of balance in their thinking, their feeling nature or their physical body, it can in time create disease and problems for the person. All those subtle nuances that you feel and think affect the chakras, for every part of you affects every other part – you are a moving, sensitive being. This is why in many of the exercises I recommend, I lay emphasis on focusing, centring and balancing. This creates a harmony between your greater whole and the various levels within you.

Interestingly enough, when you give healing, your own chakras can become involved because they represent, if you like, the vibration to which you are attuned. So, if you are dealing with somebody who needs healing on a very spiritual level, then it will be the higher chakras that will be involved. On the other hand, if you are going to give healing to someone who has a very physical condition, then the energy of the more physical, lower chakras will be involved.

I am often asked, "How many chakras are there?" And I have tended to adapt my response to the generally accepted number of seven. (Some schools include an eighth – either above the crown or at the feet.) There are actually many more. So, when healing, it is best to send a thought of balance to the whole chakric system of your patient, as each chakra needs to be in a balanced relationship with the whole. Healing the whole chakra system, you will find that your healing for that patient will be even more successful and thorough.

10

The Auric Field

Nature has a wonderful way of containing and protecting this wholeness in the form of an auric field. This is an emanation from the spirit that surrounds and protects every living being. It not only protects on all levels, but it reflects the state of that being or person, whether they are in good health, whether they are happy or depressed, whether they are calm or fearful. If that person is in poor health, is overtired, depressed or disturbed, the reflecting and radiating aura is diminished and weakened; consequently its ability to protect is diminished and weakened. That person is more likely to pick up germs or be affected by negative thought and emotions. Whereas, if in good health and happy, mentally and emotionally, a person's auric field will naturally be strong and bright and will protect efficiently on all levels.

You are a Spiritual Being

The more you can sense that you are fundamentally a spiritual being, the more your spirit will take ascendance over your personality and will have its way. You bring the wisdom of your spirit into the body and the spirit itself shows you where you are stuck, what is out of balance, where your pain is. And as your spirit hits that pain, it is like a light shining in a dark room, revealing all the hidden monsters. But once the room is in light, then there is transformation and those shadow aspects can become potential sources of growth.

The more you can become aware of your spirit and connect with your Higher Self, the more you will understand your life experience. Some of it will be painful because that is what you have been willing to undertake in this incarnation. But the extent to which you can bring the wisdom of your spirit through to your conscious mind will correspond exactly to how much of yourself you are willing to see, how extensively you are prepared to address your shadow and understand what it is trying to tell you. You can then release those energies that need to move on within your energy matrix, within the filaments of light that are you, your wisdom flowing through space. With the help of your spirit, they can be released.

Your spirit is your saviour. Your spirit is your warrior. Your spirit is your power and your love, and you need to bring these

11

through. I am not speaking about bringing the wisdom of your spirit through to enlighten just what you have learnt since you were a tiny baby in this life. I am speaking of bringing it through to enlighten that whole karmic pattern that you have brought over into this life in order to move beyond it, to move beyond the need of any particular stuckness.

Remember, it is not always possible in one short life to do what you set out to do. Things are left unresolved. But your spirit wishes for resolution. To achieve this, it needs to come down to the tips of your toes, to fully manifest through your soul. That is enlightenment. Enlightenment is not moving beyond the body, up and out; enlightenment is bringing the spirit to enlighten your mind and body, here and now. If you bring the wisdom of your spirit down through your intention, then you will have enough courage to face your fear, to absorb it and not to project it on to others. For when your intent is to face your fear, having avoided it perhaps for many years because it may have come from a previous life experience, your spirit responds to that call and comes in more closely to enable you to do that.

This is *your* incarnation, bringing your spirit into form, bringing into this shell a fullness and a beauty, a love and a truth. That is the true potential of physical incarnation. It is bringing your spirit in as fully as you can so that you then resonate with Earth itself, your spirit together with the spirit that is Earth.

Where is the Higher Self?
The Higher Self is an energy in which is centred the wisdom and experience of everything that you have ever been. A more mature person has a greater awareness and acceptance of this wise part of themselves and so is able to connect with it more easily; which is how they would be able to access the higher levels of consciousness when giving healing. In a younger spirit, that Higher Self will be outside the body. It won't normally come into incarnation but will be as an energy around the aura.

The Higher Self is like an energy in a capsule, and that capsule is part of your spirit, normally outside the body. If it is outside you might ask, 'Is it vulnerable?' And my answer would be, 'Yes, it is vulnerable.' This is why at this time in the evolution of planet Earth, we are trying to teach you to enable your hearts and minds to make that connection with your Higher Self. Let me give you an example. When someone becomes involved in some fundamentalist thinking and they become very closed in their thinking, very controlled by others rather than being in control of themselves, the odds are that the connection with that wise part of them will be weakened and consequently vulnerable to the shadow.

I don't want you to think of it as a capsule that is floating around because it is not something that is visible. It is a spiritual energy that is part of you as a whole and is part of your spirit. Even though it is outside the body, the connection is still there.

How spirits become stuck

On entering a physical body you start to lose your innocence, because the physical body is in a certain stage of evolution itself and is far from perfect, with its own light and shadow. You inherit a brain, a mind, a physical body that is carrying with it the energies of its own ancestors. So, you suddenly find you are having to cope with the energies of your father and mother, your grandparents, and your great grandparents, going right back. And this is your first experience in a physical body, having to deal with other energies that are very real ones because they are there in that physical body that you are inhabiting. How, then, are you going to deal with them?

You begin to wonder if you have made a wise choice. Maybe your father doesn't turn out to be what you had hoped he would be. Maybe he provides a very different challenge to the one you had anticipated - and your mother, too. You begin to become aware of their frustrations, their problems, how they are coping with light and shadow. Already you are beginning to feel stuck.

The reason I am telling you all this is that this is one of the very first times that the soul aspect of the spirit can become stuck in that first incarnation (or at an early stage in any incarnation), having to deal with a whole host of invading issues, and they are very invasive. The spirit is desperately trying to cope and sometimes it will retreat into its own shell. It will disconnect itself from the heart. It will separate itself energetically from the physical body that it is inhabiting. So, what will happen to that physical body, losing that vital energetic bonding between the spirit and the physical?

The physical body will start to become very caught up in the energies of its parents and this may begin to manifest as diseases associated with its ancestors. And the spirit/soul will feel out of control and totally stuck. It has choice. It can go forward, it can stay where it is, and it can go backwards. If it tries to go backwards it will call for a very early death to that body. It may say to itself, 'My goodness, I am not ready to take on physical life. It may be all right for some spirits, but not for me!' And that is quite a clear cut decision. It is OK because the physical body will die and that spirit will go back through a rehabilitation process.

But the real difficulty arises if the spirit/soul really does become stuck; it can become almost atrophied in that physical body and the person concerned will become very mechanical, very lifeless. Things will be done only because they have to be done. These people will go through life protesting, grumbling all the time, not able to reach out.

Now, if perchance the personal guide of that spirit is able to get through to it, it may enable it to say, 'I need help, I need healing' and it may draw towards it someone who can release that spirit to live more fully in its body. So, one of the areas to look for with stuck energy is where somebody is living their life in a totally automated, totally uncreative, unproductive way, very much a slave to the needs of others and what *they* want to do.

So often, people think of stuckness coming about through some kind of overriding energy, which of course it can; but it can also come about through exactly as I have described.

Trauma
Another way in which a spirit can become stuck is through an accident, a shock, a very deep trauma that somehow takes all the energy out of it. It could be through war, a catastrophe, losing a loved one, being very stressed or not evaluating its own life properly and so denying its own freedom of choice, its free will. You can see why these are very important times because on one level the whole planet has allowed itself to become stuck through control, through the power of the few dictating how people should think, how they should believe in God. These are all areas that create stuckness in spirit.

The Need for Healing

So, the stuckness that I am talking about is not just one that is limited to the odd person here or there; it is affecting millions of spirits on your planet. It needs to be dealt with through individual healing and healing circles all around the planet in which you offer freedom of choice; because the energies are ripe at the moment to take something like this. This is the time for it. What is important is that those of you who believe passionately in freedom do not become dogmatic in your own belief. You can only offer it. You cannot force it.

Here, I must stress the importance of self-discipline for when you really attempt to put this into effect you will find both light and shadow, love and fear. And because of the tribal culture of humankind, there is an unconscious fear amongst your scientists, politicians and religious leaders that what they stand for may be underwritten by other means of expression which exist on a subtle level. They fear that they may lose control of everything they believe in and so they set about to control others rigidly in order to feel safe and powerful. Indeed, many religions have a forced discipline, with punishment, sometimes a very severe, torturous punishment, if you don't follow the rules.

Interestingly, to gain control over others is to contact the shadow side and I'm going to make a very dramatic statement in saying that any organisation whether it be political, spiritual, corporate or whatever, that is seeking control at the expense of those who follow it or are part of it, can only be working for the shadow.

So, you have to impose your own book of rules, your own code of conduct, your own understanding of where you are and where you need to be. This means recognising your own vulnerability, facing your light and your shadow, and that means moving beyond condemning others. It means moving forward with an unconditional view of love and all-being.

Fear

Spirit stuckness can also come about through fear that causes the individual to retreat into him/herself, and perhaps become involved with psychic/spiritual exercises, forms of meditation even, that encourage stuckness by closing the mind, closing the heart, closing the spirit. In mentioning religions, I am not just talking about religions as you would understand them. I am talking about archetypal stuckness where you become caught up in a belief – it can be philosophical, it can be political.

To free yourself means dealing with the fears in your heart, in your being, it means sitting back and looking at your life and saying. "What can I do about it?" and then understanding that there is a great deal you can do about it. You can stand on top of the highest hill and reach out and feel that cosmic energy coming down. This is the moment when you realise that you are responsible for your own life, your own journey, your own direction. When you really face your fear and understand its origins, you can release it, let it go and move beyond it. Releasing stuckness requires vision and understanding.

Planet Earth is desperate for spirits that are stuck to be released and I hope that any organization involved will recognise that they need to do whatever they can to create a new energy throughout the whole planet. Yet, it isn't a new energy, it is really contacting God energy in the most loving way.

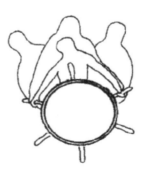

Chapter 3

BASIC KARMIC HEALING

With basic Karmic Healing you are accessing divine cosmic energy and transmitting it to a client through one of the many different techniques practised in the world today. Remember, that true healing comes about through transformed consciousness.

Karmic healing is concerned with bringing the wisdom of the spirit, the Higher Self, into closer communication with the soul and hence, the mind of the client, strengthening the connection at the crown chakra and the solar plexus, the two areas where the spirit connects with the mind and the body.

This may be done by using channelled cosmic energy in a direct way, or through using guides, symbols, prayers and so on. The energy is then received by the client, helping their spirit to find balance and harmony on the many levels within themselves, thus enabling a self-healing to take place. This may be felt on the physical, emotional and/or mental levels.

So, Karmic Healing focuses on healing the soul aspect of the spirit in relation to the mind and body. It is very much concerned with what your spirit has brought into the physical body, the wisdom and understanding gained from all past life situations, and from every other experience prior to those past lives. For your spirit had choice from the moment that it was created, even choice as to which branch of evolution it wished to experience through, all branches of evolution being complementary to each other and not spiritually superior or inferior to any other branch.

Having chosen the evolutionary path of a human being, what your spirit brought in when you entered your physical body at the moment of conception was not only light, but shadow, your past unresolved issues as well as your resolved issues. You chose your parents for the challenges that they would give you. You chose your environment and you chose the body that you inhabit. If life is difficult, you might well question that choice. But remember, your spirit may choose challenging situations for its own purpose even though, once in the body, the physical mind rebels.

In giving Karmic Healing, you are helping to create balance and harmony in the energy flows, enabling the person on an emotional level to deal with those issues that are difficult to face. Through this, the spirit is able to connect more closely to the mind, body and emotions. This is the type of healing that most healers use.

What is Karma?

A great deal has been said on this question of karma which has tended to confuse the issue. Some people even find the concept of karma a convenient excuse for many things. If they can find no answer to a question or situation they are apt to say "It is karma!"

So what is this elusive thing? Is it a law? A blueprint? Let us examine it together. I say 'together' for the knowledge is within each one of you and I am going to release it in order that you can recognise and collate your own thoughts in a progressive direction.

Karma is a plan. You might say it is a plan of your life, a plan of your friend's life, a plan of your Earth planet, of everything around you. But how far does that plan go? Where does it begin and where does it end? What determines the plan?

Let us consider the last of those questions first by explaining that karma incorporates the law of cause and effect. The karmic plan of a spirit is no haphazard collection of events but is to a great extent determined by the sum total of that spirit's previous experience. Once free from the body, a discarnate spirit is able to look back over its entire evolutionary experience to date and, as a result of this, determine the sort of Earth existence it now wishes to undergo. Some of this karma or plan will arise as a direct result of the spirit's previous life, but if a wise choice is made it will also be a complement to its overall evolution.

So, to me, your future karma is not predestined or pre-determined. Your future karma is the result of the decisions that you make at any one moment, not only in your incarnation but in your spirit existence. In that sense, you create your own karma, in and out of the body.

The Karmic Blueprint

When a spirit is discarnate it is not limited by time or space as you are on Earth. Let us say that it reaches a stage of understanding in which it is ready to incarnate into a physical shell. It seeks to establish a body which it feels is going to give it the form of experience it needs. For instance, a particular spirit might realise that it requires to experience as a sailor who will be drowned at sea. It will be helped and guided by higher spirits to choose a suitable body that will provide the necessary experience it is seeking. Because that spirit is not bound by time and space it can look along a life and discern the path it will take. It will not see the details of that life but it will see the milestones, the important events.

The spirit learns that in this particular life it will run away from home and go to sea – that it will not marry but will meet up with a close friend from a previous life and see the world – that it owes this friend a debt of gratitude and wishes to repay him in some way, and so on. Having ascertained the plan or karma of such a life it would enter that body at the moment of conception. Each one of you has a karma of your own life and it is up to your individual free will as to whether or not you fulfil that karma.

The free will a person possesses stems from the spirit. Each individual spirit chooses its own way to evolve and there are an infinite number of ways of evolution. No two spirits have ever trodden an identical path of evolution; each chooses its own individual path to fulfil its karma. This choice is made by the spirit exercising its free will outside the body, before incarnation, because once it has been born as a person here on Earth that person is subject to prevailing laws, environment, world conditions and many other factors that create certain limitations to the expression of free will. This is the challenge that a spirit takes on when it incarnates: to express itself within the limitations of the physical body and prevailing environment in which it finds itself, whether it remains in its country of origin or moves further afield.

Karmic Patterns

Remember, you chose your physical body before you entered this life. Having incarnated, you still have freewill to choose the finer details of your experience for, indeed, you have the choice to make the best or the worst of your incarnation, to fulfil it or to let it drift aimlessly; and you are making that choice every day of your life.

I am now going to make a statement regarding karma which may come as a surprise to some of you. A spirit *could* complete its entire evolutionary karma in one life, although this would be very exceptional, or it could choose to do so over a number of lives, tens, hundreds or even thousands. This it chooses of its own free will. Here I am referring to the overall karma of the spirit and not the particular karmic facet it elects to face in any one Earth existence.

It could be said that on average a spirit would take six to ten incarnations to ascend to a higher plane but spirituality is not really something you can work out in a specific way for it is so individual. Some spirits may take many incarnations and others very few. If anyone tells you there is a fixed number of incarnations for a spirit to undergo they are misleading you. It is up to each one of you to fulfil your evolution in the way you are best able.

Similarly you will meet the person who has returned to pay what is termed a karmic debt for a wrong or harm perpetrated in another incarnation. He can work off this karmic debt in the first five years of his life or it can take him a lifetime. He may never complete it in the life in question; this often happens, in which case his spirit will have to return and re-live those karmic experiences in yet another incarnation.

As seekers you may ask what we can do about it. "How can we know if we are fulfilling our karma?" The first lesson is very simple, so simple that you will say, "But we know that already." My answer would be, "If you know, why don't you do it?"

The first lesson in anyone's life is to learn tolerance and under-standing. Two simple words which mean so much and yet seem almost non-existent as I look around your Earth planet today. That is where you start, in your attitude to those around you. At the same time you learn to see yourself for what you are and this is the hardest test of all. There is hardly a person on your planet today who truly knows himself, although some can go quite a long way towards it.

Stop for one moment and look at yourself fairly and squarely. What do you see? Cut away all the things you would like to be and think you are and look at the real you; for you are what you are, no more and no less. If you can do that honestly you will then be able to see your friends and neighbours for what they are and, in accepting them as they are, this will help both them and yourself. Having reached that point you will move forward steadily and progressively in balance and harmony.

You came to Earth to experience such things as are available on this planet. A part of this experience is to seek spiritually. On one hand you are evolving in a body which is limiting, but on the other hand you are following the unlimited path of spirituality. All these things fall into the unfolding of your karma and, in pursuing a balanced life and following the dictates of your true conscience, you will flow *with* the laws of the universe and realise your karma.

Karma and Healing

Let us look at karma in relation to illness and healing. Does healing affect karma? Yes, it does. But - and it is a very large but - it need only do so in as much as you as individuals wish it to. For example, if when you were in spirit you realised that in your next incarnation you would gain some useful experience if you suffered from a certain disease. You came into this life and eventually you caught that disease. Suppose we healed it, would that be denying you your karma?

My answer is a very simple one. If, in taking that healing, you can place it in a proper perspective, understand why you are receiving it and know that God does not wish you to suffer, then it is possible for you to rise above the necessity to suffer. If you can appreciate all this and use the benefits that you receive from such healing to help other people, then you will not only have achieved your karma, you will have learnt a greater lesson than you would have done from having the disease and not being healed. This is what is termed 'transmuting your karma.'

Indeed, there are some cases in which the healing of a disease by spiritual means is part of a person's karma, for such an experience can open one's eyes to a broader understanding of the universe.

Your Earth planet is fast approaching a period in its evolution when physical suffering will be less prevalent. Spirits wishing to atone for karmic debts will either elect to do so in service to their fellow men, or choose to incarnate on another sphere that is passing through a period in its evolution in which suffering of a physical nature is still being experienced.

In our healing we use thought, for in its power there is unlimited scope for mankind to heal diseases and disabilities and to help people to adjust their lives. The higher, the finer, the more subtle level the healer seeks, the more power he will be given to work with. I believe that such is the will of the Father/Mother God. If we go into the world with this knowledge and understanding we can help people quietly and kindly.

The subject of karma has many aspects and side issues. I have tried to give you an overall picture of my teaching on this subject and hope that you will gain from it a deeper understanding and an enrichment of your own life and the lives of those around you.

Healing, not curing

At this point it is worth remembering that healing is not about curing, in contrast to orthodox medicine which is based on symptoms it attempts to cure. Healing energy needs to be used to enable the patient to become more conscious on the physical, emotional, mental and spiritual levels of the right way forward in his/her life.

Soul Healing with Sound

Many hundreds of years ago, soul healing - here I am deliberately using the term 'soul' - was quite a simple procedure. It involved the healer, the teacher, the one who was aware, to speak a word and that word resonated through every room in the house of the soul. It went beyond the intellect. It was the *sound* of the word that was so important, not so much its structure. It was the *sound.* In the uttering of the sound there was a release within the soul. The soul was more able then to unfold, to release the channel and to be in connection through those communicating pathways with the greater part of the spirit.

Some of you are now working with sound, which truly is a very powerful tool for healing at that soul level. Unbeknown to you, with the instrument of your voice you bring through a very delicate vibration, an energy that comes through when the voice is uttered. Accompanied with unconditional love, the vibration can heal another soul. It is important for you to recognise that your voice is a powerful tool and that when you make your spiritual connection, when you move to the outer edges of your being, you allow these vibrations to come in. It is a tool that can enable you to touch another human being; you are unaware perhaps, but it is there. It can unlock the door in the soul and the soul can then bring in more of the wisdom of the spirit, enabling that person to live their life in a more fulfilled way.

EXERCISE 1. Healing Karmic Patterns with Sound

If you work as a healer it is equally important that you heal and work on yourself as well, by cleansing, balancing and protecting yourself – in other words, getting yourself into a balanced condition before you give your patient healing energy. If you sense that, within you, something feels out of place or is pulling you into the past, then you can do this self-healing exercise.

Focus on that feeling within you for a few moments and then let go of your thought and allow yourself to expand to the outer edges of your being, so that your spirit can enter more fully into your soul. For that is where your past is, it is in your soul. Allow yourself to hear a voice, a sound through your soul, a voice calling for your spirit to come in, into that soul level where some of the past energy has become stuck. Allow yourself to hear that sound and hold the energy for a few moments, before gently letting it subside. Then realign and re-centre yourself.

EXERCISE 2. General Self-Healing Exercise

Breathe in deeply, in a harmonious and relaxing way. Feel that divine energy sweeping in, integrating the different levels of energy that comprise you as a total being, yet allowing you to become aware of those different aspects of your being. Now, I want you to go gently back in your mind over the past year and remember any tensions, fears, anxieties, any issues that have given you problems throughout that period.

Gather them into one container, it can be a box, a bag or a sack; because each one of those issues, those fears and feelings of inadequacy, have stemmed from the past, not the present. And, in a sense, it is all those attitudes and the feeling of being put down, of not being worthy, all those kinds of negative feelings, that are truly your friends; they are your teachers, your enablers, for they are enabling you to step forward by pointing the way. So, as you fill your container with these negative fears, I want you to put them in with love, with gentleness, but with firmness. Then say:

"I am part of these as they are part of me. I am shifting them into this container because, although they have provided me with a platform with which to learn, they have chained me to past fears and have stopped me from going forward."

So, in filling that container, you are not rejecting them, you are not punishing them, you are acknowledging and releasing them, and drawing strength from the fact that you no longer need them as an inhibiting quality in your life. . . Doesn't that feel good?

I want you now to look at that container and ask yourself: is it real or imaginary that it seems to have started to shrink in size? Allow it to shrink. Allow it to get smaller and smaller. . . and smaller . . . and smaller. . . How does that feel now? Has it disappeared for you yet, or is it still there? There is no right answer; don't worry, you have not failed if it is still there. But you need to be aware in your mind of how it is. There will be a remnant there, because I have only taken you back one year.

Now, this time, I want to take you right back to the moment of conception. Feel yourself floating back, feel your physical body getting younger, feel the tightness around your spirit as you come back into childhood, where the spirit may feel inhibited, pressed in and not allowed to be what it would like to be . . . Feel the strength of some of those disappointments, that disillusionment and bewilderment. What do you want to be when you grow up? Are you going to make a mark in the world? Or, are you afraid you are going to be useless? The threat of competition, the lack of under-standing from those around you, how you needed the space in order to become your own being. . . Those dreadful adults who always knew better than you and were too scared to stand back and allow you to be what you are! How does that feel now? . . .

We are going back again even further, to being inside your mother's womb, right back to that moment of coming into the physical body. This time you have quite a large container in which you are going to put all the unwanted baggage of those years. . . Then as you come forward again as a baby, as a child, as an adolescent, coming into early adult life with all those hopes, aspirations, disappointments – a lot of baggage to put in that container, this time, isn't there? . . . So, once again, put them in with love, release them, let them go; yet allow yourself to under-stand that on one level every experience in your whole life has been as it was, it has been necessary and part of your own evolutionary development.

Have you now filled it with all that you no longer need? Allow it to shrink to a manageable size and then lift it, filling and expanding the space beneath it with unconditional love. Up it goes, fired by that love, up into the universe - into the Sun, or an appropriate symbol, to be transformed.

When your spirit came into the physical body at the moment of conception, it faced the challenges and traumas of that coming together, of that fusion in which you brought with you everything you had been, together with the energies of your own ancestors, which have become part of you now in the physical body, the influence of the archetypes with which you have been associated, and the need for releasing and letting go . . . letting go! . . .

"This is me, I am me! I am ready to face the rest of my life with a smile, with an understanding, with a vision. I seek unconditional love. I move beyond the judgment of others, of myself. I allow myself to forgive both others and myself. This is my life, I am my life. And now, I love my life!"

Slowly regain the reality of this present moment, the reality of your physical body and all the different aspects and parts of you that make up the whole. "I accept what I am, no more, no less." Become consciously aware of the room around you and the chair you are sitting on. You have gone back and come forward at the same time, in order to accept where you are. Open your heart and your mind, your whole being.

Finally, centre and ground yourself well into your body.

Chapter 4

PREPARE YOURSELF FOR HEALING

As a vehicle for channelling healing energy, the following simple disciplines will enable you to maintain balance, wholeness and health, acting as a catalyst for others in the healing process.

I am giving you the following guidelines to help you prepare yourself for the act of giving healing energy to another. It is really important that you channel healing energy from a state of poise and balance within, for in this state you will be far more receptive to the healing energy of the universe - God's energy, cosmic, divine energy - and your healing will be greatly enhanced.

It is also important to take responsibility for your healing by protecting yourself and your client, and ensuring that you do not pick up the condition of your client. The following exercises will offer you several different approaches to preparing yourself for healing.

EXERCISE 1: Cleansing, Balancing and Protecting.
This requires a three stage process, involving *cleansing, balancing and protecting* yourself and, if giving healing, you may like to use it with your client. Details of these three stages are as follows:

Cleansing with a Sieve
Sit down (or you may prefer to stand) and relax. Visualise a large circular garden sieve which you hold between both your hands. It has a mesh that can sieve out whatever your mind determines.

Starting beneath your feet, bring the sieve up slowly through your subtle bodies, chakras, physical body, mind and aura, sieving out, in your mind; firstly, any unwanted physical ailments, cells, etc.; secondly, any unwanted feelings or emotions and thirdly, any unwanted thoughts and psychic dross. Bring the sieve slowly above your head. As you do so, imagine that you are closing a trapdoor above your head in order that the contents of the sieve cannot re-enter your being.

After closing the trapdoor, empty the contents of the sieve into a bag, seal it and send it off into the universe (the Sun or an appropriate symbol), to be transformed into positive energy. It is important that this is done with a loving thought.

Repeat the exercise three times, each time using a sieve with a finer mesh. The last time, the sieve's mesh will be as fine as a coffee filter.

If you prefer to sieve downwards from the head to the feet rather than upwards, that is your choice. You might also like to sieve yourself on three levels - the physical, the emotional/mental, and the spiritual.

Balancing

Choose a suitable visualisation to balance yourself. This can be done in various ways:-

- Hold your hands together as if you are praying. Hold them fairly low so that you can feel the bottom of the palms of your hands pressing together tightly. You will feel yourself coming together, realigning on all levels.
- Imagine you are focusing a camera lens, bringing the picture into sharp focus. That picture is of you as a whole person, with each part of you (subtle bodies, chakras, mind, physical body and aura) in complete alignment.
- Imagine that you are seated with an overhead projector (OHP) in front of you focussed onto a screen. You have 7 transparencies, each one in a colour of the spectrum with red being on top, on which there is an outline drawing or photograph of yourself. . . .

Switch the OHP on.

Place the red transparency on the OHP first, projecting a red outline or photograph of you on to the screen. Red represents the Base Chakra with its focus: 'The will-to-live.'

Next place the orange transparency on top of the red, making sure that it sits directly on top of it. Orange represents the Sacral Chakra with its focus: 'Procreativity and balance.'

Then place the yellow on top of the orange. Yellow represents the Solar Plexus Chakra with its focus: 'The emotions, positive and negative.'

Then green on top of yellow. Green represents the Heart Chakra with its focus: 'Altruistic love.'

Then blue on top of green. Blue represents the Throat Chakra with its focus: 'Expression and creativity.'

Then indigo on top of blue. Indigo represents the Brow Chakra with its focus: 'Intuitive thought.'

Then finally, violet on top of indigo. Violet represents the Crown Chakra with its focus: 'The will-to-be.'

Check that all the transparencies are aligned together perfectly so that only *one* outline remains which, because it is made up of all the colours of the spectrum, will be *white*, a radiating white light.

You have now brought your aura and all your different levels of consciousness into sharp focus. You will feel integrated, harmonious, and 'together'. When you are in total focus and balance, with your auric field surrounding you, strong and bright and healthy, you will feel in complete charge of yourself and your life.

Protecting
Visualise (imagine) a golden sphere with a cross in the centre. As this is a sphere, the cross will need to be multidimensional. In your mind, reduce it until it is the size of an atom. Place it in the centre of your body, in the area of your solar plexus or heart.

Slowly and gently enlarge it until it encompasses the whole of you. It will make you feel very comfortable and protected. You can, in your own mind, adjust the size of the cross and sphere so that it encompasses the whole room that you are working in, your car, the house you are living in and so forth. It will also protect you against malicious thoughts and negative energies as, being a golden sphere, it will merely reflect those unwanted thoughts straight back to their source.

It is also important to surround this golden sphere with a white energy encompassing unconditional love, forgiveness and respect. Thus, if someone sends some malicious thoughts in your direction, they will be returned to them with unconditional love. This is very powerful, for the one thing that the shadow cannot handle is unconditional love.

You can of course use other symbols, ones with which you feel more familiar.

Out of the Body?

When you are giving healing energy to a client, you are also responsible for the protection of that person; for if, during the process of your healing, they allow themselves to leave their body, it increases their vulnerability. It is better for your client not to go into an out-of-body experience, unwittingly or willingly. So, when giving healing to a client, make sure that you work within a suitable protection.

Do not pick up your client's condition

Last but not least, so as not to pick up your client's condition, there is a very simple visualisation you can do which I have used and recommended for many years and I have never known it to fail.

Imagine that the healing energy is passing through your body and, as it leaves you, it passes through a one-way valve such as you have in a car or bicycle tyre. The healing energy can then pass through you, but you cannot draw anything back.

Finally, when you have finished giving healing, remember to centre yourself again and check your own auric field.

EXERCISE 2: A Meditative Approach

Relax, breathe comfortably and release any tensions on any level. As you breathe in, lighten yourself and feel that you are drawing in the finest cosmic divine energy. Feel that energy filling and relaxing every part of your physical body, coming down through your head, releasing your forehead and face, relaxing your shoulders, your arms, hands and fingers, your spine, your thighs, your legs and your feet.

Feel the energy touching and relaxing every organ within your body, your heart, your stomach, your spleen, your liver, your intestines. And a final breath to relax your whole body. Say to yourself, *"This is my physical body, and I have aligned it with my whole Self."*

Drawing in cosmic energy to connect with your mind and your nervous system.

With each breath, draw in cosmic energy and feel it subtly, gently infiltrating all the different parts of your nervous system. Feel it soothing, connecting every cell within you, making you whole. Say to yourself,

"I am at one with my heart and my mind. I feel the cosmic energy in tune with every part of my body, my spirit and myself as a whole being. I hold my physical body and my mind in balance, I am in balance."

Drawing in unconditional love energy to uplift your emotions

On the in-breath, feel the energy of unconditional love freeing your emotions and allowing them to flow. It is a most wonderful feeling if you allow that energy to flow through you, so that it can synthesise with your anger and enable you to say:

"This is my passion, this is my need to fulfil my life. How can I use it to help the universe? I feel it stirring my emotions, so that my love for myself and my love for the world can become unconditional, knowing in myself that I AM LOVE and that I need to extend that love to others."

"I feel through my emotions a whole range of the shadow: the fear, the guilt, the inadequacy, the not being good enough, the rejection."

"I also feel through my emotions, my own sense of honouring and accepting myself, my self-empowerment, knowing that I have something to give myself and my fellow beings, knowing how I can use emotions to stir my imagination and access my intuition, aligning myself with my psyche. This allows me to channel God's energy so that I can be what I am, no more and no less."

Stay with that experience for a few minutes and say to yourself:

"I feel my emotions. I love and honour my emotions. I allow my emotions to integrate within my whole being".

Moving to the fourth dimension which is that of your spirit

Try to become conscious of your spirit, your essence, your Higher Self which communicates its finer wisdom through its incarnate aspect, your soul; for your soul is that part of you which is in the 'now', in your life as it is. Acknowledge your Higher Self for it holds your latent wisdom and potential for fulfilling your karma in this lifetime, for bringing forward your mission and allowing it to permeate every aspect of your life.

As you breathe in, you are drawing in divine healing energy, it is filling your spirit and your soul. Allow it to touch every level of your being, your mind, your emotions, your physical body. Say to yourself:

"I honour my spirit, it is my spark of God, my connection with the Godhead. It holds all my past and all my present and, by being in contact with it, it can enable me to steer myself into the future with confidence, with trust, and with an inner knowing."

"I am my physical body, I am my emotions, I am my mind and, at the highest level, I am pure spirit. I am one integrated being and all my chakras and subtle bodies are at peace. I am filled with unconditional love and I am at peace. I offer this peace to my client, and I shall intuitively know what type of healing they need: it may be Karmic, it may be Advanced Energy Healing, Concept-ional, Homoeopathic, Ancestral, Archetypal, or a combination of more than one of these."

Now you are ready to attune yourself to your client and to give healing in whatever way you practise, remembering to begin the healing offering – for it must always be an offering rather an imposition – with the words, *'If it be thy will'*, meaning, *'If it be the will of the client's spirit'*. And remember always to realign and rebalance the client after any healing session, building and strengthening their aura. Finally, re-centre yourself, strengthening your own auric field.

Chapter 5

ADVANCED ENERGY HEALING

As we move into the coming age, so our approach to healing needs to change. Consciousness is energy aware of itself, so a greater sense of personal responsibility is required with regard to the use of the mind and the flow of psychic energy.

I now want to introduce a finer, more subtle form of Karmic Healing which I shall call 'Advanced Energy Healing'. This could be broadly termed psychic but it does, in fact, differ from the more regular forms of psychic healing. It is the positive application of the power of thought to those imbalances that are the true cause of all disease, both mental and physical. The principle is as simple as mind over matter, but like all simple things it is only by practice, experience and understanding that the fullest benefit can be obtained from it.

The energy healer learns to use his or her mind as a transformer for those cosmic forces that exist throughout the universe, about which your scientists delight in telling you in this day and age. Thought power is no longer an hypothesis, it is an established fact. Thought can destroy; when wrongly used it can cause psycho-somatic disorders, breakdowns and many mental illnesses. I teach people to use the other edge of that sword, the side which builds, mends and puts matters right.

Thought sounds a vague enough thing in itself, but do not imagine that the utilisation of thought force limits one to a control of the nebulous and etheric. A healer who is capable of transmitting a certain form of power can indeed effect great physical changes such as the dispersion of unwanted tissue and the healing of bone conditions; bearing in mind that, ultimately, the body itself actually does the healing, although the healing energy will speed up the process.

The Power of Thought

The power of thought is infinite; indeed, it could be regarded as the law of the universe. The Godhead, all the different forms of evolution, the people existing in the various solar systems, the animals, physical matter throughout the cosmos, all these in their infinity owe their very existence to the power of thought.

Every aspect of human life is the result of thought – philosophy, art, science, all forms of invention, healing and indeed, life itself – for are we not all thoughts of God? You see, my friends, the Godhead itself is but supreme and infinite thought or intelligence. Thought influences your life from birth to death. There are many things in the world today that could be achieved by the potency of thought if man only knew how to use this great gift.

I have instructed many in the art of healing the body and the mind, but these powers are no secret, for the technique lies in the harnessing of the power of thought. Every human being is capable of using thought positively to a greater or lesser extent, the only limiting factors being ability, innate wisdom or evolution, and knowledge of how to use that thought-power. In other words, nothing and no one else can limit you except yourself and your own attitudes of mind.

The universe itself is thought existing on many different levels from the finest to the densest. The amount of the universe you yourself can conceive is infinite in so far as you are able to broaden your thought to accept, understand and comprehend it. You can use your mind to tap into this power which exists throughout the universe and, from the universal point of view, the extent to which the power of thought can be harnessed is limitless.

Harnessing and Directing Thought

Upon your Earth planet, at various times throughout its history, there has been a great deal of nonsense talked about the secrets of the universe. These are not petty rituals nor are they some mysterious knowledge only attainable by a few. As I said, the secret of the universe is the power of thought. Consider for a moment that if it were not for thought none of you would be responding to these words. You could not do one thing in your life if it were not for thought; you could not eat, drink, sleep or walk. The majority of diseases of the body and the mind and, in fact, the majority of all Earth problems today are due to the lack or misuse of thought force, for this is in itself a negative power and, as such, becomes potentially just as strong a force as the more progressive, positive thought force.

Over the ages, a great deal of ritual has been used in esoteric work, but none of this is necessary, as the same results can be achieved by the power of thought. It can be used to help all forms of life and assist in bringing a greater balance to the planet, in order that all beings learn to express themselves with love, tolerance, humility and understanding towards their fellow beings. One has to think clearly and strongly and direct one's thought positively, in harmony with the flow of the cosmos.

As you direct your thought, waves are sent out - call them vibrations, if you like - and these waves travel through the ether into infinity. Every sound or thought which is made is recorded for eternity in infinity. So you can imagine that when, for example, during a war a force of hatred is set up, it can have a powerful effect on the enemy. This is a negative use of thought-power/psychic energy and if used deliberately, will rebound eventually on the sender(s).

THE YANG PSYCHIC AND THE YIN PSYCHIC

In contrast, healing energy workers harness the power of thought with very different motives, sending out positive thoughts of love, healing and protection. Consider these waves of thought. When they travel indiscriminately into the universe they tend to become diffused if they are not channelled into a definite direction. But a trained mind can direct thought into a beam which can maintain its strength until it reaches its goal.

Some words of explanation here. Accepting that everyone is psychic to some degree and that everything has a polarity, this psychic energy flow can be expressed in one of two ways: either receptively, as an inflow, or positively, as an outflow. I have chosen to adopt the terms 'YIN and YANG' to describe this polarity as it is expressed in different people's psyche. The YIN psychic is predominantly like the radio-receiver, receiving impressions, messages – the medium, the artist, the intuitive, the creative person who follows their intuitive imagination. The YANG psychic is predominantly like the radio transmitter – the healer, the protector, the therapist, doctor, nurse, carer, the performer etc.

Those of you who use psychic energy, will find that you can express it more easily one way or the other; and it is helpful to be aware of which comes more naturally to you so that you can optimise your ability. One of the things I want to make clear, however, is that while a person may be extrovert in their character, this does not necessarily mean that they are yang psychically. It has nothing to do with the personality. It is whether they psychically *affect* their surroundings as in healing, or psychically *receive* inspiration, awareness, intuitively. Some people may find that they are very strongly yang or very strongly yin, while others are nearer to a mid-way mark. All who work with psychic energy need to develop the opposite flow as well as what comes most easily to them, so as to maintain a balance. It is all about finding balance, because the more balanced a psychic person is, the more effectively they can use their thought power/psychic energy as the higher levels become accessible.

Remember, however, as I said earlier, psychic energy must only be used in harmony *with* the flow of the cosmos; in other words, with unconditional love and respect.

WARNING: *Beware* of using thought power/psychic energy for purposes that flow *against* the flow of the cosmos, that is, for egotistical or manipulative purposes, for this will rebound on you sooner or later.

Both yin and yang psychics have their vulnerability – the yin psychic can become very ungrounded; and the yang psychic can become too focused and blinkered. But together, they work well, each contributing their own strength. I know of many couples who have benefited from this dual approach which can be very effective in dealing with negative energy.

Sometimes the yang healer will need the yin input in order to interpret a disturbed atmosphere or person when dealing with a particularly negative situation. However, it is the yang energy that is needed for clearing a space or a person.

On the other hand, when a yin psychic goes into trance, or is channelling, and is in that vulnerable state, the yang healer offers support by projecting and holding a containment such as a sphere of light which surrounds and protects the channeller. (This should not be too strong as it might prevent the yin psychic from picking up a spirit wishing to communicate. Rather, a fine but firm visualisation, with the thought that only spirits of light may enter.)

When the yang healer uses their outgoing energy to clear negative, stuck or invading energies, they need to remember that whatever is cleared must also be helped and healed, as it needs as much assistance as the person or situation involved. *(The type of techniques used for this are taught on the courses provided by the Spirit Release Foundation and the College of Healing. Details of these organisations are given at the end of this book.)* And the void that you have created in that patient, place or situation, by clearing, must be filled with unconditional love - maybe using a symbol if you wish - for 'nature abhors a vacuum.'

You can see that there are complementary impulses at work here: one has a more detailed intuition, while the other is able to use a stronger ray. Together they create a balanced polarity and this, in itself, gives an added protective strength.

As we move into the Age of Aquarius, it will become more and more important for the yin psychics to be the receivers of higher energy, and they will need yang psychics to keep an eye on them; because when you reach for the light, you can also attract the shadow. It is very easy then to lose control and unwittingly attract the invading energy to yourself. So you need to work with, preferably, a yang healer to support you and make sure the area of protection is efficient, effective and safe. I would add that this person does not necessarily need to be present. It can be done remotely.

The Responsibility that comes with the use of Thought Power

One of the biggest problems on your planet at this particular time is that people are out of alignment, in the sense that the different aspects of their being are not resonating harmoniously together. If a person has a physical problem there is usually an emotional/mental issue causing it, or perhaps a spiritual issue dating back to a past life or lives. This is becoming a very significant issue and if we are going to move towards bringing in peace and understanding and bridging the gaps on your planet, there needs to be much more attention paid to people working together on these advanced techniques of healing.

The power of thought then can be used for healing the body and mind by clearing away accumulated negative thought forms and bringing the spirit, the subtle bodies and the physical body back into harmonious alignment and balance. Once this is done, the body is then able to heal itself.

Each spirit has free will, which means it has choice; but it is living in a society on this planet that is heavily conditioned by the media, by religion, by corporate business. So it is becoming increasingly difficult for spirits to exercise their own free will because they are persuaded that this is the 'right' thing to do, the 'right' thing to eat or drink or the 'right' way to behave. At the end of the day, the spirit inside that person needs to have the freedom, the clarity and the strength to make a decision that is coming from its own inner level of being.

Those who are entrusted with the gift of using this thought-force must always recognise the Ultimate with humility and obedience. So great is this power that it could be used to quell riots and disturbances, it could be used to stop a war; but it must always be sent in the right direction and not used for evil or selfish purposes. It must never be used to override a fellow being or even a creature from another form of evolution. As I said before, he who feels tempted to send out negative thoughts with intent to harm another – thoughts that work against the flow of the cosmos — will draw the full force of the Law of Karma to rebound upon him. Jesus understood this in all its depth; he said simply, "As ye sow, so shall ye reap."

The powers of the universe are of themselves neither good nor evil, they are simply forces; it is only the use made of them and the intentions of the individuals concerned which make them black or white, selfish or selfless, evil or good.

Disciplines for the Healer

Is it necessary to condition the physical body if one wishes to harness the power of thought for healing and allied purposes? In my opinion it is essential that the physical body be kept in a balanced and fit condition, which means inner and outer cleanliness and a light diet that discourages the lower forces. This involves, if possible, abstinence from any form of red meat. I appreciate that people have their lives to lead and today, especially when one sometimes has to eat in public restaurants, there is often little choice. But for your own safety as a healer and psychic, I would advise you to observe this discipline if you possibly can, for red meat lowers the density of the body and the blood content encourages entities of the lower astral.

For a reasonable period before working - and by that I mean at least twelve hours - abstinence should be observed from any form of alcoholic drink. It is also advisable for any members engaged in this work who are unioned with a partner to abstain from sexual functions for a similar period before using thought-force in a positive and directed way.

With regard to drugs, these should never be touched by anyone involved in this type of mental discipline. I will be dealing with the drug question and the detrimental effect drugs can have on the evolution of the spirit, in detail later on. I am, of course, referring to the hard drugs and hallucinogens, although I also consider that even stimuli such as coffee and tea taken frequently are not exactly aids to spiritual or physical development!

If all these points are observed, then there will be no danger and the psychic workers concerned will be able to maintain a high standard. Some of these disciplines may seem unnecessary, but I can assure you that, when you are entering more subtle dimensions, the slightest defect can attract a multitude of undesirable influences. They are not impositions but suggestions designed to help you to protect yourself and to go forward without fear. After taking every point into consideration I know you will agree that, irksome though they may sound, they involve little sacrifice when compared with the spiritual upliftment and fulfilment you will achieve from the help you will be able to give others by observing these suggestions.

Further Thoughts on the Auric Field as Protection

As I have mentioned before, the aura is an etheric substance emanating from the spirit that surrounds the physical shell and acts as a case or covering for it, thus protecting it from all cosmic forces. If the physical body and its counterpart, the etheric body, had not this protective robe/force-field, they would be open to influences of all natures and would certainly not survive. The human aura can be opened voluntarily by thought, or involuntarily out of psychic curiosity or by shock, and anyone aware of this can learn to keep their own aura well closed, again by thought.

A person's control, doorkeeper or guardian angel - call it what you will - helps to control the aura of its charge, especially in sleep, so that as little harm as possible can come to that body. A balanced mind and healthy body will help to maintain a strong and healthy aura.

When a person's aura is open or out of alignment, all substances of a malevolent nature may enter. A sudden physical strain or jerk can serve to cause an opening, such as in the case of an accident where a leg is broken or flesh injuries sustained. Cases of disease involving viruses, germs etc. can soon be brought under control by realigning the physical and etheric bodies and sealing the aura, for such particles of life cannot exist unless they breathe from the ether; in fact, they live on the impurities in the ether.

It is also possible to cleanse the aura and the body to a certain extent by the use of a cleansing ray. Medical science has found that the use of bandages and artificial forms of sterilisation is effective in cases of surface wounds, inasmuch as they give the aura time to adjust itself while the natural healing processes take their course. By the use of the power of thought, the energy healer seals the aura in the affected places, so that the resident impurities will die from lack of nourishment and can be dispersed in the normal manner. This speeds up the healing process.

The aura acts as a protective barrier against thought vibrations that are travelling about in the ether. Were it not for its existence, every human being would be completely open to all thoughts and expressions that have been uttered throughout the history, not only of your Earth planet, but of all other planets and solar systems in the infinite universe. Of course, this does not happen, firstly because there is this auric barrier and, secondly, because the human body and mind are not sensitive enough to receive these impressions and thoughts.

This inevitably leads to the question of how mediums receive communications; surely they must open their auric barrier? This is true, for when a medium enters a state of genuine trance there is more to it than relaxation and bodily conditioning. The medium must learn to sense the presence of an entity, challenge correctly so that only those spirits that are working for the power of Light may present themselves and, finally, open the aura to allow the communicator to enter. As mentioned earlier, I also teach yang healers to protect the medium, again by the use of the power of thought, when any work of this nature is undertaken; and also to challenge any nearby spirit with the medium, to ensure that the spirit is what it claims to be.

The Advanced Healing Process
Since the whole basis of our energy healing is thought, it is not essential for the healers to touch their patients at all; any movements made with hands are only done as a form of directive for their healing power and to aid them psychologically in concentrating their thought to the best of their ability. When most people give healing, the energy will come through the hands, the fingers and the palms of the hands; and if you are going to touch the patient, you need to have their permission, under laws of litigation. I will make no 'shoulds' or 'oughts' on this. However, the best way for you to heal is the way that feels right for you, and if that involves touching the person, holding their shoulders or arms, whatever, fine. But you don't *have* to touch the person for healing to be effective.

All diseases cause a maladjustment between the physical and etheric bodies and until this is righted the physical condition will not improve. If the sufferer is a strong willed person he may be able, with assistance from his spirit, to put right the maladjustment, but in most cases the services of a healer will greatly speed up this rebalancing process.

Cancer

Diseases such as cancer are brought on by friction between the physical and etheric bodies, caused very often by severe emotional stress or a physical or mental shock. When this type of experience is not 'healed' at a deep level, it can cause a weakening of the auric field through this friction. Very often it is a cry for *change* on the part of the spirit of that person. Here again, the physical condition is unlikely to improve until this is understood and implemented. Also, cancerous parts have a life force of their own and this needs to be dealt with by an experienced healer or, sometimes, the determined will of the patient, before healing or surgery can effect a cure in the long term. *

Advanced energy healing is an in-depth process. Suppose someone comes to you and says my arm is dislocated. When you direct your healing to that person you are not just directing it to that dislocated arm, you are asking the spirit/soul what has caused it; why has it happened; what was it in them that drew it towards them; and why do they need to go through that particular karma? You are directing the healing to the highest possible level of understanding within your patient and, for this, it is first necessary to attune yourself to that higher level within. Only then can the patient's energy, through resonance, also attune within to help them to connect to their own higher levels of understanding, wisdom and being.

You are healing primarily on a spiritual dimension but the thrust of the healing will then filter down to include the mental, emotional, etheric and physical dimensions; because all these different aspects of your being need to be integrated into a whole and sometimes it is necessary to start from the top and work down. So, you lift the energy around yourself and your patient onto the highest, finest, most subtle level and then channel the energy appropriately to bring that person into balance, into sharp focus, and into a sense of ambience in which they can connect between the various levels.

EXERCISE: Spiritual Acknowledgement and Protection

I would like to offer you now a form of what you call psychic protection but which I prefer to call spiritual acknowledgement; for the more centred, harmonious and at peace a person is, the stronger their auric field will be. And remember, the auric field is their natural God-given protection.

Relax yourself and breathe in deeply. . . and as you breathe in feel that you are drawing in cosmic energy, that divine energy . . . it is filling every part your being . . . and as you breath out, release any tensions in your body.

As you continue to do this I would like you to look within your heart, to feel the energy there. . . isn't it beautiful? . . . And, from that heart energy, feel your thoughts, your mind, going right into that inner part of you, that wise part. . . . feel that innermost part of you coming together with your soul, making connection with your Higher Self, so that your spirit feels complete. . .

Now, through that state of consciousness I would like you to feel the link reaching right up to the Godhead that created you. . . . Allow it to transform upwards, for remember, you are trying to tune a low voltage into a high voltage, a comparatively dense frequency into the finest frequency. I want you to feel that link extending upwards. . . . Can you feel that? It is there for you, it is denied to no one - can you feel it?. . . . Hold that feeling within you and allow it to permeate throughout your whole being . . . on every level . . . .total love. . . . .

Now, gently return to your body bringing a part of that God energy with you that is yours; because as long as you acknowledge God, that highest power, that Ultimate Thought, you are still joined to it on that finest level. So draw back down to yourself that part of your own God energy. . . . feel it merging inside you. . . . you can feel that?. . . .And as you feel it I would like you to say to yourself:

"I honour, I respect, I love my whole being. . . a total being that reflects my light and my shadow . . . and in that reflection I honour, I acknowledge, I respect my physical ancestors and thank them for the physical experience they have given me. . . .and I release them! . . . I acknowledge the archetypal energies that my spirit has been involved with, both in and out of incarnation, which now sometimes hold me back and create an aura of stuckness within me. . . I say to those energies: I honour you I

respect you . . . . I release you! . . . .for I am now ready to move on having learnt from you. . .

"And finally, I honour and acknowledge myself as a free spirit of the universe. . . and in that freedom I link with that part of the God energy that is mine by right. . . And I allow it to shine through my whole being, thus giving me a protection, acknowledging my individuality, acknowledging my uniqueness, acknowledging my vitality. . .

"I LOVE AND ACCEPT WHAT I AM, NO MORE, NO LESS."

As you feel those energies around you, once more become aware of your physical body, thank it for the support that it has given to you in this life, the opportunity that it has provided for you to move forward to face new challenges and old challenges. And now, centre and align yourself, feel the ground beneath your feet and come right back into your own reality.

I accept that this is a form of protection that you cannot take lightly, for it needs to be done in great seriousness, in great peace, in great harmony. But, with the type of challenges that are beginning to emerge, this is the level of protection that you now need. I offer it as a blessing. It is there if you wish to try it for yourself or for a client. If you do, I think you will find it immensely rewarding.

> *We would recommend that in a case such as this, you ask*
> *for assistance from a healer/therapist connected with the*
> *College of Healing or the Helios Foundation.*
> *(You will find a further chapter on Cancer on page 118.)*

Chapter 6

CONCEPTIONAL HEALING

The moment of conception is a moment of opportunity,
allowing the spirit to continue its journey through
another physical body, with its challenges of light and
shadow arising out of what has gone before.

To me, birth is the transition of the spirit into the life of the body, and death is the transition of the spirit back from the body into the life of spirit. When a spirit decides to come into a physical body, it does so with guidance. However, every spirit has choice, free will to choose which way it will go and whether to accept or reject that guidance.

Out of the body, the spirit's free will and choice is much more open than it is within physical existence because, once incarnate, both the body and the environment place constraints on its choice. So before incarnating, it will make its choice in a thorough way, whether to be born to rich or poor parents, into a highly technical space or a primitive nature space. It may choose a body that is healthy, or one in which there is much disease; it may even choose to be part of an accident or war, because it wants to sacrifice itself to create a lesson or an example.

The spirit has its own reasons for its choice of incarnation, what it wants to achieve and the challenges that it wants to set itself, even though the physical mind may rebel and find life hard to accept. Indeed, finding your true direction in life can be a difficult challenge in itself. The wise spirit will choose challenges that it feels it needs.

When a spirit comes into incarnation, it has come out of the spirit realms where it has been resting and seeking and growing in understanding. Having decided once more to face physical incarnation, and having taken a deep look at the type of experience it is seeking and the challenges it is prepared to meet, it will concentrate its energy sending out a particular frequency, as if to say, 'This is what I am looking for'. Somewhere, two people who are going to conceive will reflect that energy, and so the spirit is drawn to them because the energy they radiate is very specific and reflects the spirit's needs. It may choose parents whose spirits it has lived with before; on the other hand, it may choose parents who offer a totally different form of experience.

The decision to take on another physical body is not an easy one for a spirit to make, because out of the body it is free and it knows very well that in going into that physical experience it is going to feel restricted.

Just imagine that you, a spirit, are as free as air, and suddenly you find yourself in a sort of underground tunnel, being drawn into a vortex of energy. Sometimes a spirit, because it is vulnerable, will shriek and scream and say, "No, no, I'm not ready, I don't want this!" It may have regrets about its choice of parents and come into the womb, in fear, in dread, in anger and rejection, knowing that it has chosen to give up its freedom for another experience within physical living. But, you see, once that spirit has made that decision and the seed is fertilised, it is drawn in almost like a suction and it is very difficult for it to draw back.

The Mother

When I talk to you about the parents, you must understand that what I am describing to you is a model, and that there is no right or wrong way for two people to come together to conceive. There is only what happens. Let me give you some thoughts.

Let us say that the mother is not expecting to conceive. Maybe she thinks it is the wrong time. Perhaps the sexual act has been forced upon her and she finds she is pregnant, so she has to make some big choices. Does she stay with that pregnancy, or does she abort the child? The only way the mother can truly find the answer to that question is by tuning into her deeper self, looking at her circumstances and at the needs of the spirit and its potential life.

Where the mother knows that to give birth to that child would not be right for her or the child, I consider that abortion would be completely justifiable. If it is being done because the pregnancy is the result of casual sex without the intention of procreating, then the decision must reflect the needs of both parents, otherwise the resulting child, or spirit if it is aborted, will carry a heavy burden and may be very resentful. On the other hand, if an abortion is carried out in love, then the spirit may welcome it.

You must understand that once fertilisation takes place, the spirit has started to experience. It may well be that it experiences all it needs inside the mother's womb in a few hours, a few days, a few weeks. In the culture in which you have been brought up, you are used to thinking that living to an old age is what matters. Old age and the length of a life are immaterial to the spirit. In one life, a spirit may experience all it needs to fulfil its karma in five minutes; in another, it may live for one hundred years and still not find a level of fulfilment.

Abortion - is it right or wrong?

I am often asked whether abortion is right or wrong. I cannot answer that question because I do not believe in right and wrong. I only believe that the spirit does what it needs to do at any one moment in time; that if pregnancy is terminated, taking into account all the circumstances that can arise - emotional, mental, situational and environmental - then that is how it is, and one has to acknowledge that maybe the spirit wants it so.

It can also be that while the mother is carrying the spirit inside her womb she is very angry, she doesn't want another child and is angry against the person who has made her pregnant. So she directs her anger, fear and resentment into that child. And of course, mixed up in that resentment could be aspects of ancestral issues, archetypal and karmic issues.

Perhaps the mother doesn't take responsibility for carrying the child, she doesn't want the restrictions of being pregnant, so she carries on drinking or smoking or leading a life that in itself is an unspoken rejection of the love and care that the child needs. I say all this without judgment and criticism, for when a mother is in that state, my heart bleeds and goes out to her. She needs support and love, wisdom and help.

Abortion has been condemned by various religions as bad or wicked, because the leaders concerned do not understand the various options that the spirit may choose. The abortion can actually be inspired by the spirit because it sees no other way forward. It may have come into that fertilised seed and realised that it was not ready to incarnate, or that it has made a wrong choice and feels compelled to find a way out. There is very often a difficulty between the spirit and the fertilised seed that it has incarnated into, and it is through that difficulty being communicated to the mother at a deep level that the need for abortion takes place.

Abortion is not about killing the spirit; it is about enabling two spirits, the mother's and the child's, to move forward in freedom and in love. It can be a blessing rather than the opposite.

If the mother harbours a sense of guilt, she can be helped to communicate inwardly with the spirit of the child, to 'hear' what it may wish to convey and respond to it in whatever way she feels appropriate. This allows for a more spiritual and fulfilling ending to the brief relationship.

The Father
Now, let us consider the father - why is he choosing to perform the sexual act with the mother? If both parties are doing it to release their emotions, that is fine, but in my opinion it is proper that they should use some form of contraception. I am putting this carefully because it is a very radical statement. I consider that contraception is fully justified unless the two people concerned are wishing to conceive a child. *It is the responsibility of that couple.*

The ideal situation for fertilisation and birth is where there is a deep love behind the sexual act, a spiritual love that needs to project itself into creation. Of course, one has to acknowledge that fertilisation sometimes takes place by accident; however, it is the love between the two people that is the key factor.

Where is the father in this? What sort of responsibility is he taking? Does he want the child? Does he want to have the sexual act with other women? Is he really in love with this person? Is he accepting the responsibility of being in love? *For being in love is a responsibility; it is about two people acting towards each other in an unconditional and responsible way.*

So, then the spirit comes into incarnation to face what the parents have to offer it. It may be love. It may be fear projected through overprotection and possessiveness. It may be anger and resentment; perhaps the child is not of the sex that the parents wanted, for there are many cultures and individuals in the world who wish to have male or female children at certain times.

Finally, the greatest moral that is coming out of this is the understanding that if you wish to have children, offer it up to the cosmos, and go along with the process of your own love and your own need. It is equally important to understand that no woman or man *has* to have children. If you choose not to have children, that is fine.

It is a great challenge for a spirit to be incarnate on this planet now, at a time when there are considerably heightened energies, for these are increasing the metabolism of the body. They are also affecting people's emotions and particularly their need to fulfil their love for another person through the sexual act. So the need for the sexual act is increasing and this is bringing out the shadow side of sex. *If a child is created out of the shadow side, that is a tremendous challenge for it to face.*

Releasing Disturbances at Conception

Conceptional healing relates to the moment of conception when the seed is fertilised. When a spirit enters the body at that moment it is the sum total of all it has been, bringing all the resolved and unresolved aspects of its being, choosing parents that are going to enable it to meet the challenges it needs. That particular moment draws together different factors, both the issues which the spirit brings and those of both parents.

Going back in awareness to that moment of entry, of conception, can allow a tremendous release from some of the issues that have created trauma in a person's life from the very beginning; and the healing of that moment can enable a level of understanding and acceptance of an individual spirit's mission which had previously been beyond reach of their conscious awareness.

Conceptional Healing enables the spirit to release:
- the emotions experienced at the time of fertilisation.
- the emotions experienced and acted upon by the mother and/or the father.
- all the musts, shoulds, coulds and conditions that have been laid down around childbirth by various cultures, religions and political organisations.

In the eyes of God, men and women are equal, each offering different qualities; for the woman has within her both the male and female, and the man has both the female and the male within him. The spirit itself is androgynous and will sometimes choose to incarnate into a male body, sometimes into a female body. It needs both those experiences. Equally, there is also the need to understand both sides of one's persona whichever gender the spirit is currently manifesting physically. So a man needs to become aware of his feminine aspect and not deny it; and a woman, likewise, needs to honour her masculine side. And, of course, both need to be aware that balance and harmony are the two key words to spiritual wholeness.

EXERCISE: How Conceptional Healing can be Facilitated
A client can be helped in Conceptional Healing by first understanding how the healer is going to facilitate and the reasons for it. It is important to gain the full consent of your client. A cautionary warning: when you carry out this type of healing the results can be very cathartic, it can be like a sudden explosion of trapped energy that has been there for that person's whole life.

It is especially important with Conceptional Healing to guide your client into a deep relaxation such as is described in Exercise Two in the chapter, *Prepare Yourself for Healing.*

Different healers may wish to work in different ways:
- To facilitate the client's regression gently back to the birth experience, then back inside the mother's womb, and then further back to that moment of conception, so as to enable the release and expression of trapped emotion. When you do this, you will need to hold your client in your healing energy with unconditional love and total allowance for the spirit of that person to be released from the trauma of their conception. It is important that words of release are repeated three times for it is like a challenge, but a challenge with love.
- To project him/herself back to that moment of entry of the client's spirit by tuning into their energy, sensing the type of experience and emotion, and then enabling the client to release that which has been withheld - again repeating the release and affirming it three times.

- To use a process of visualisation, perhaps telling a story or metaphor which will evoke the moment of conception. While the story will not reproduce the actual circumstances, the subconscious mind can translate the metaphor into the context of that moment when the client's spirit incarnated. Thereafter the healer can enable a release of emotion.

For example, the story might be of a seed that is cast off a large sycamore tree in the wind and spirals to the ground, then finds itself engulfed in the darkness of the surrounding soil and wishes to return to the freedom of being part of the tree and able to experience everything at a great height. It painfully realises that this is not possible - there is no means to go back. The soil is cold and damp and the seed is aware that it will not provide adequate nutrients for its growth in the months ahead. What does the seed feel now? Enable the client to amplify that feeling into their consciousness, and then allow release three times. Elements of the story can be elaborated upon as appropriate. The client will need careful grounding back into the body after this type of experience and help to integrate the healing process.

It may become apparent that the client's parents, whether alive or dead, are in need of unconditional love and healing; in which case, Conceptional Healing can lead to the healing of parents and ancestors, combining perhaps other types of healing described in this book as appropriate to the unique and individual circumstances of each client.

Twins

Sometimes more than one spirit is drawn into incarnation and twins, triplets, and so on, can result. When this happens the relationship between those spirits is usually very harmonious, but it can sometimes bring to the surface unresolved issues that persist during their lifetimes. One may feel crowded out by the other(s), vying for attention and love as they grow up. One may be favoured by either or both parents, creating jealousy and/or resentment.

When twins are born it usually occurs because two spirits that are evolving closely together enter at the same time through choice. There is often a very close psychic relationship between them.

If two spirits are *very* close in spirit, it can cause a mutation which you call Siamese twins, where their physical bodies are attached in some part or parts. When they are detached from each other surgically, the outcome is not only dependent on the physical skill of the surgeons, but also on the needs of those two spirits. If they don't want to be separated, they will try to prevent it happening successfully. If two twins are going to be separated in this way, it would be very helpful for them to be sent healing at that time to enable them to reach a decision, because Siamese twins are created out of indecision; it is an unclear boundary and becomes an unclear birth.

Sometimes, ordinary twins are not in harmony with each other because of disharmony between the two spirits. If there are two spirits present at the moment of conception, both wanting to be the one to incarnate, the force of their dual energy can create a division into two embryos, which can happen when both try to enter the same fertilised egg simultaneously. If those spirits are really confrontational, then there may be a still birth, an abortion or a miscarriage - something could happen to terminate the incarnation of one or both of them. Alternatively, if the twins are born, there will probably be difficulties in their relationship during their lifetimes.

You see, it is possible that because those two spirits are stuck in the womb and cannot see a way forward together, the strength of their energy somehow communicates through to the mother's emotions and mind and creates the need for an abortion. So, I repeat that I find it very sad when I see people condemning abortion without understanding all the issues on a deep level.

Where there is a problem between two twins, it could be very helpful to give them Ancestral Healing to ease the tension.

Chapter 7

ANCESTRAL HEALING

Along with your karmic or spiritual inheritance, you have a physical inheritance through your ancestors and DNA to come to terms with, releasing what no longer serves you well. For then you will be able to see yourself as a whole, independent being, loving and honouring yourself for that beacon of light that is you.

A Spirit's evolutionary Choice

I would like to share with you some more thoughts about your ancestors. When a spirit comes into incarnation, it does not necessarily do so in isolation. Individual spirits are born into the universe to experience, having first been created by the Godhead and, during that very early formative time, they begin to develop their own flavour and essence as they move through various planes of pre-physical existence with choice and free will. They are searching and this draws both light and shadow towards them, as they begin to come together in groups.

When they feel ready for physical existence they will choose a form from any branch of evolution manifesting within the universe in which they have been created. If they choose your own planet, they would have the choice to incarnate into any of the kingdoms on Earth: mineral, vegetable, animal, or human, or even into the elemental kingdoms of earth, air, fire or water.

I would like to make it very clear here that, in my perception, all forms of physical life on Earth are complementary. One branch of evolution is neither better nor superior to another. They are all different and they all complement each other. It is very important that you understand this for, if man decides to try and interfere with the chain of complementary evolution, he will create negative energy, in fact he will create the very situation he is trying to avoid.

Soul Groups

Although a spirit incarnates individually into physical existence, it is usually part of a soul group. These are spirits who, through association, have become familiar with each other's energy and output, with each other's frequency and feeling/sensing energy. As the spirit evolves, so does physical matter evolve. Nothing stands still and if you try to make it stand still, it will become stuck, stagnate and turn in on itself.

When you come into the physical body at the moment of conception, you will choose your parents because of the challenges they will provide for you. You will not necessarily incarnate alone, other members of your group will probably incarnate at around the same time. Not at precisely the same moment or year, but perhaps within a span of fifty years or so.

As you start to evolve within the physical body, you meet others who are from the same group experience as yourself. There may be an instant deep recognition and you feel that you have known them before. Sometimes you will meet someone from another group with whom you have a feeling of confrontation that may even burst into violent action.

Each time you incarnate, you are trying to take a step forward in your understanding, in your wisdom. You bring with you the sum total of everything you have been, the light and the shadow, the resolved issues and the unresolved issues.

Physical inheritance

The physical body is an incredible inheritance, not to be ashamed of or rejected, for each human body has its own beauty, its own uniqueness. When you speak of it in this way, you begin to understand the implications of what you call cloning which, in my opinion, cannot ever totally succeed. It may succeed on one level, but you will not be able to recreate the wholeness; and true spirituality is about wholeness. It is about cleansing the spirit and the body, and understanding the depths to which spirit needs to go, through the dirt and degradation that sometimes the physical body has to face. For when you debase the physical, you debase the spiritual.

On the level of spirit you are the sum total of all your previous experience, incarnate and discarnate. On a physical level you have inherited the genes of your parents, of their parents and so on, the result of many, many thousands of years of handing down DNA through procreation, and the living out of physical existence. So when your spirit starts to handle the physical body through the medium of the soul and the Higher Self, it has to contend with the physicality of the body, the genes that have been passed down from your parents, from their parents and from all your forebears going right back through the centuries. You are entering a physical body directly related to its own ancestors and the attitudes that have come through from them.

The integration of the spirit and the body is an essential part of evolution for it is the coming together of two streams: the spirit's experience and the body's inheritance. True spirituality is found in the balanced blending of the two, in togetherness. On the spiritual level, this integration is about the coming together of the light and the shadow, again a balanced blending of the two.

DNA energy
There is a kind of sheathing around the DNA, although not carried by the DNA, which encapsulates all the moods that have come down through physical life: the anger, the joy, the frustration, the hopes, the expectations, all of which release different chemicals into the body and which, of course, reflect aspects of the parents and the antecedents. This can sometimes relate to the types of illness you may develop.

Each time a child is conceived, it is not only carrying the genes of both parents, it is carrying the physical angst of those parents. It may be carrying generations of fear, of anger, of revenge, of retribution. So when you meet a person who is very aggressive, it may be not only the karma of their spirit, but also the inheritance of their genes.

Sometimes, through an ancestral blockage, violence emerges, because the double influence of that blockage together with the need of the spirit becomes unbearable. It creates resentment and it can create bitterness against parents, for deep down there is a subconscious knowledge of what has been passed on through their genes.

Ancestral healing is something I would recommend everyone to do and, for children, you would need to adapt it accordingly. It is part of your overall self-healing and, in the process, your own DNA energy shifts and that resonates with and affects those who lived before you and those who live after you. As you deal with issues in your life, some of them will connect with your ancestors and some with your spirit's karma; and here I am separating the karma of your spirit from the karma of your family, although in some instances, they may well coincide.

So, in sorting out your own DNA you are affecting your children and their children, going forward seven generations. In other words, the influence is cleared. You are also affecting the spirits of your parents and your ancestors who are journeying elsewhere in the universe, going back seven generations. They will feel the benefit of what you are doing. It affects the past and the future for when you heal yourself, you do indeed affect the planet!

It is because the planet is in this present dynamic stage, that those thereon are able to deal with their issues in this way, and with this effect. So, it is a wonderful moment.

The Choice of a Body

Sometimes a spirit will choose a physical body whose parents provide not only the challenges it needs, but also have the matching energies coming from past physical lives. So a spirit, in reincarnating within its own group spiritually, may also reincarnate within its own group physically. When you look at your physical body as it is now, you may well have incarnated previously into the same family sometime in the past and be carrying some of the same genes: the implication being that you may be related to your own ancestors!

In addition to handling your physical body, you are having to relate to the energies of your parents and of the people with whom you come into contact in your life. If you make a choice where that relationship is compatible, you will bring forward all the plus energies of both the past incarnations of the spirit and the ancestral inheritance. However, as your spirit usually chooses parents who provide a challenge, this can mean that your physical body also provides a challenge. This can sometimes be overwhelming, possibly creating difficult situations in relation to health.

Ancestral Healing versus Karmic Healing

Ancestral Healing relates to the history of your body and those aspects that have been brought into your environment by the thoughts, actions and deeds of your ancestors; as opposed to Karmic Healing which relates to the history of your spirit. To perceive them as separate, frees you to have a clearer understanding of your karma, for as you relate to others - to siblings, children and parents - you also have to relate to different aspects of yourself. This is an essential part of the spiritual unfoldment as you move into the Age of Aquarius. It is about acknowledging the divine within, developing self-empowerment, and a realisation of all those different aspects which relate to finding spiritual clarity.

When a person becomes ill or has what you call a dis-ease, it can be spiritual, it can be karmic, it may be emotional because the emotions provide the balance between the spiritual and the physical; or it can be physical or environmental. Yet, if it is one, it is also all of these things. Any true healing has to come from that understanding, acknowledging yourself as a whole being, loving yourself as a whole being.

In the case of adoption it is important that ancestral healing goes back to the birth parents. Remember, also, that Ancestral Healing is particularly concerned with negative characteristics that have been passed down. The true affinity between spirits is not lost, for unconditional love has no ties.

It can be much more difficult where there has been the donation of sperm because the line has been obscured. Humankind is unwise to play around with these situations because it obscures the pathway. In the case of someone who is in that position, it would be important that the healing went back to the donor. It has to go back to the actual birth parents. If you give this type of healing to someone and it does not appear to work, it may be because they have not told you or they are not clear about their birth parents.

There are many ways in which Ancestral Healing can be conducted. I have tried to simplify it, to allow it to be more easily applied. If a person has pain, hurt, or repeated patterns of unwanted behaviour within which he or she may be giving out or receiving, and they have not responded to the normal forms of healing, they may well respond to Ancestral Healing.

Ancestral Healing Exercise for self or client.
(If for a client, pause after each exclamatory phrase, gradually increasing in intensity where indicated.)
Prepare yourself for healing (see Chapter 4).

Breathe out fully and then breathe in deeply and on the in-breath, feel pranic energy filling every part of your being. As you breathe out, feel your body relaxing, releasing any tensions, coming closer to your essence within. Centre in your heart.

Breathe in again and feel that divine energy filling your whole being. Breathe out, letting go, letting go of any inner tension.

Breathe in, once more feeling that cosmic divine energy filling your heart and your whole being – breathe love into every part of your body.

As you breathe out, feel your spirit coming closer to the physical.

As you breathe in, draw in that universal divine energy once more and as you breathe out, feel yourself bonding together into one whole being.

In that feeling of oneness within the physicality of your being, become conscious that you were created by your father and your mother. You are partly your mother and partly your father, physically, through the genetic DNA energy they have passed on to you, which is contained in every cell of your body. Become aware of yourself and those aspects you have inherited from your parents. . . Feel the energy of your genes reach out and touch each of your parents, becoming aware that at this moment you are living because of them. Hold that feeling within yourself.

Now reach up through your mother to her parents . . . and up through your father to his parents. Your thoughts are now going out to six people . . .parents and grandparents.

Now reach even further beyond your parents and your grandparents to their parents. Feel that your DNA has reached back to fourteen different people who have created you. It doesn't matter that you do not know who they were, because you are working back through your own DNA, and your own sheathing to your DNA, to all the attitudes and tensions you have inherited, all the doubts and fears that have come forward, the putting down, the sacrifice, the system. It is helpful to think this process back through seven generations.

Finally, speaking slowly, and deeply from your heart, say out loud, "I acknowledge you! . . . I honour you! . . . I release you!" . . . Again, "I acknowledge you! . . . I forgive you as I forgive myself! . . I release you as you release me!" And a third time, "I cherish and love you! . . . I honour and respect you! . . . And now I am moving beyond my inherited karma and I release you. Release! . . . Release!! . . . Release!!"

Slowly withdraw your energy back into your physical body. Feel yourself as you are, the sum total of everything you have been, both physical and spiritual. Feel that you have moved beyond the need of any stuck ancestral issues. Feel them draining right out of your body . . . right out of your body . . . right out of your body!

If you should feel any pain or discomfort in any part of your body now, enshroud that pain in unconditional love. Place the pain in a golden bubble and allow that bubble to go out into the universe. In so doing, it goes back to all the circumstances which have created it. On one level you are releasing it. And on another level you are helping those who were involved in the original cause of it because you are offering them unconditional love which contains forgiveness, harmony and wholeness.

Look inside yourself and fill the area where there was pain with unconditional love and new loving thoughts such as compassion, acceptance, gratitude, whatever feels appropriate for you, with maybe a colour or a shape of your choice.

Having released the ancestral attitudes and tensions, you may wish to affirm the separation of negative and positive traits in the following way:

Once again feel the energy of your own genes. Feel that you are sieving that energy so as to separate the parts that you wish to integrate, from the parts that you wish to release. As you sieve out the energy you wish to release, you do not necessarily need to define it. You are sieving the energy of each one of your genes.

Take the energy that you have sieved out as no longer needed, thank it for the part it has played in your life and let it go.

Now take the energy that you would like to be part of you, and allow it to course through every part of your being from your fingertips to your toenails. Feel that energy coursing through your head, your arms, your trunk, your legs and your feet. It will feel like an energetic shower of energy! It can make you feel younger, it can make you feel vital, it can make you feel dynamic, and it will have affected your DNA. It can take you forward into the next stage of your life.

In your mind, create a symbol that incorporates your own energy of the present and the future, so that you will be able to identify this energy in the future. . . Now breathe in that symbol and feel its energy filling every cell of your body and every aspect of your being. Say to yourself,

"I honour my present . . . I honour my future . . . I cherish my past because it has brought me to where I am now . . . and now I release my past . . . I am my present!"

Finally, centre yourself, close down and ground yourself, and gently return to the here and now.

What is most important in this exercise?

It is the understanding behind it, the acknowledgment, the love and forgiveness, and the sense of finally letting go and being let go of by the past. For some people it may be necessary to do it more than once and in a way which is specific to their individual needs.

As I perceive it, Ancestral Healing is about removing stuckness. If you have a very stuck past, it brings you into this life with a rigidity, where you are perhaps frightened to look outside your own much bounded vision. When your spirit has been stuck for a long time in this way and is then released through Ancestral Healing, you can suddenly find that you feel like a loose cannon, and you need to rebalance and harmonise within yourself.

It is rather like a ball made up of twisted wires, twisted energies, which has become so stuck and tight that it cannot move. Someone comes along and says 'There is a small bit here that is ready to make a move, so we'll help it on.' Suddenly that tight ball starts to become lighter because that small part has moved on, it has created space. Instead of the tight knot, there is now room for things to be loosened, to move around.

When Ancestral Healing has been given it is important to follow it up with regular Karmic Healing, regular balancing, re-aligning all the levels, to give the spirit a chance to regain control. For the spirit that is trying to control the universe that is you, suddenly finds it is no longer captain of the ship. Although previously the ship was going through some quite murky waters, at least the captain seemed to be in charge, even though he wasn't sure where he was steering the ship. Now that tight control has been taken away and he's trying to rediscover where the wheel is and where the tiller is; it needs a great deal of gentle healing to re-orientate the self gradually, so as to regain control of the ship, a very beautiful ship which can have a beautiful voyage.

This type of healing also provides an opportunity for you to re-evaluate your qualities and abilities, the things you know deep down you can offer; and it requires you to have the confidence to allow them to surface.

GROUP HEALING EXERCISE: For an Individual

Let us take an example in which there has been violence as part of the make-up of people within a family background, which has never been resolved. It has been passed down from generation to generation, perhaps for centuries. Ancestral energy can be carried forward in this way and create a blockage in a person's life, especially if they are not aware of how to handle it. In the case of adoption it is important that the healing goes back to the natural parents.

The following exercise needs to be carried out only by healers who are proficient in clearing negative energy. This is not an exorcism as such where an alien spirit is attached, but a clearing of accumulated ancestral negativity. The group prepares itself for healing and one person undertakes to lead the healing session.

Group Ancestral Healing

The client or healee needs first to be very aware of the particular quality or angst, be it fear, anger, jealousy, that they feel they have inherited from their ancestors. Where do they sense that angst in their body?

The healer then enables the healee to think of their genetic energy containing that particular negative quality, reaching back to their parents, their grandparents and so on, back through to their past ancestors, as in the Ancestral Healing exercise. They need to feel that negative quality reaching back through their distant ancestral line.

The healee is asked to bring all the angst that has been passed down through the generations into the present moment, by drawing it into their body and holding it. They may see it as a shape, an object, a colour, or just an intense feeling.

With a strong, positive healing energy, the group of healers then encapsulates the angst, lifting and releasing it right out of the person, while the leader explains their actions to the healee.

Gently but firmly lift the negativity out so that it leaves the body in a myriad of stars and goes out into the universe, directed by thought into the sun or into a symbol, to be transformed. It may not be bad energy in itself, it may simply feel negative in the way that it has come together within the person.

Immediately re-centre and protect the healee and then let the healer, who is leading take hold of their hands and say:

"With the help of the Father/Mother God (or suitable arche-typal or angelic energy), we speak to you and every aspect of you that has ever been, and we clear this past pattern from your present incarnation. . . We clear the past . . . we clear the present . . we bless you!"

(Repeat these three directives twice more.)

Gently release the hands and give healing to help the client feel centred and composed. Allow them to settle for they may feel a little weak and a little light, as if part of them has been cut away. Further healing and balancing over a period may be required to restore wholeness.

AN EXERCISE TO TAKE CONTROL OF YOUR LIFE

This mental exercise can be carried out with any person, alive or dead, or any situation or negative state of mind. It is non-judge-mental, seeking no blame. It enables you to deal with feelings of disempowerment and release them from yourself, so that you can gain control of your life; and it will not affect any genuine love or affinity between yourself and another person. It deals only with unwanted negative ties and will free not only you but also the other person or spirit.

The exercise is in two parts, **A** and **B,** which can be practised simultaneously.

A.   Find a comfortable chair and spend a few minutes relaxing your physical body, breathing in deeply in a relaxed and easy rhythm.

Visualise (imagine) two circles that are just touching, horizontally or vertically.

Place yourself in the one nearest you, and surround yourself in your favourite colour. Place the person, situation or negative state of mind, in the other circle and surround him, her or it, in a colour of your choice.

Now imagine you have a laser beam that you can direct and control with your mind. Trace the laser beam round the circles in a figure of eight, completing it 9 times.

Do it at least twice a day until the circles begin to part.

Continue doing this until the circles have naturally parted and stay apart.

B.   Write a letter to the person, situation or state of mind (in the case of a person, not to send) in which you express fully what you feel on every level. It is helpful to include 10 good things and 10 not good things, and it is important that the letter contains all that you want and need to say – however dynamic! You may wish to write it over a number of days or even weeks, adding to it as your memories and feelings arise.

When completed, find a quiet, private place and prepare to read it out aloud. As you do so, use your physical body as strongly as you can to express any anger or frustration – stamping and waving your arms and fists, and banging on a cushion if you wish – getting it right out of your system on all levels.

When you have read it out aloud three times and feel that you have really released all stuck and not-OK feelings - burn it!

Case study of a personal Self-healing Process

As a healer and counsellor I began to attract clients who had autism, I was aware that this condition disturbed me very deeply, but at the time I wasn't sure why. I knew all would become clear.

During a meditation, which had as its focus Ancestral healing, I tuned in to my ancestral line. The issue was on my mother's side of the family. I saw an image of my mother and standing behind her were her parents and behind them their parents and so on. I asked if there was anyone in that ancestral lineage that could help me. A woman stepped away from the rest of the group, she was holding the hand of a little boy who was four years old and suffered from autism.

I spoke with her and she said that in that life, six generations ago, she had been my mother. The little boy was myself in that life. The sense of relief I felt at the time was tremendous, although it took a couple of days to integrate the awareness. This was the beginning of a long process of healing and understanding.

In that life, my mother and I had been very close, she seemed to understand me in a way that no one else could and after her early death in childbirth, I was put into an institution. I felt totally bereft, alone and unable to communicate or relate to the world around me. I later realised that in that life, I had died from an asthma attack at fourteen years of age. (Recently, in this life, I had a severe asthma attack, which did not recur after the Ancestral Healing session.)

I sat in meditation and thought about the issues that were unresolved from that lifetime and called out from each individual cell in my body the negative energy that related to that life. I sent it off into the centre of the sun where it dissolved. After asking myself for an image to replace the negative energy, I imagined each tiny cell receiving the image and sensed them all expanding with love and life. I felt a profound healing was taking place.

The Ancestral Healing had lifted the energy into my conscious mind to enable me to move forward, not quite in the way that I expected, but in a way that enabled me to understand why I had always felt so withdrawn, isolated and confused in this present life. I do not have autism, but I do have an autistic spectrum disorder, Aspergers Syndrome, and as distressing as that has been to understand and accept, with all the inevitable idiosyncrasies and difficulties, I know that it is what I have chosen in order to, not only heal the past life, but to find the gifts in what has seemed an impossible scenario. The healing and subsequent inner work cleared the locked-in negative energy relating to that life. I have left behind an inner world that I was unable to talk about and have become a teacher of meditation, an inner world I love to talk about!

Note: My research over many years into Aspergers Syndrome, particularly the work of Tony Attwood, has shown that girls in particular often slip through the net, having the ability to cope with their difficulties by copying or mirroring other people. In my opinion, healing comes about through enabling a person to express themselves, to find their sense of self and to fulfil their potential in an atmosphere of love and acceptance.

Healing needs to be offered gently and in a way that shows respect for the inner wisdom of the person; criticism and judgement cause untold pain and suffering. Allow the person to open up and unfold like the petals of a rose, to enable them to treasure their inner beauty, enable them to be themselves.

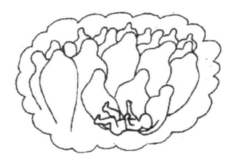

Chapter 8

HOMOEOPATHIC HEALING

Small is beautiful – and can be powerful.

The need for subtlety

As we move forward into the new millennium, more and more energy is being released onto the planet to help in the transition from the Piscean Age to the Aquarian Age. This increase of energy is not because the Godhead has said it is time it was released, but because humankind has prepared the way with its concept of the new millennium. In other words, you are setting the scene that enables us to deliver more energy. But the increase has to be understood, digested and handled. It is the heralding of a new age of spiritual understanding, looking for the divine energy within in order to find it without. It is going to be a very dramatic transition because we are coming out of an age that has been very emotional, of the emotions, into an age which is much more mental, of the mind.

The advantage of Homoeopathic Healing is that, being very fine and focused, it helps to rebalance the cause of the problem, rather than just alleviating a symptom; and for this it requires a very sensitive preparation, given here below. However, one of its limitations is that it needs to be offered on a one-to-one basis only, and should not be used for any healing sent collectively to many people.

This healing modality is to be used when the person or client has a deep understanding of where they are and how they are, but is unable to see a way through to find a healing for themselves. Because what you are doing with this form of healing is opening up something within that person. It is a healing that is completely from within, rather than from without.

The 1% Fine Potency

As in homoeopathy, in which a finer frequency of the energy of a substance is more powerful than the substance itself, in Homoeopathic Healing, the healer uses a 1% fine potency of healing energy, which makes it more powerful - a bit like a laser beam. You adjust your thoughts as you channel and guide the healing energy. When you give healing in the normal way, you draw in cosmic energy and use yourself to transmit that energy through your being to the person you are trying to help. But, with Homoeopathic Healing, instead of channelling that energy and passing it on, I am suggesting that you approach it with this homoeopathic concept of a finer level of frequency. I have used the word homoeopathic because in itself it is highly descriptive and can harmonise with the finer levels of frequency of the patient more directly.

The reason that I'm coming forward with these different and various forms of healing, is that as we enter the Age of Aquarius, the approach to healing will become more intellectual, of the mind. Therefore I am trying to pre-empt that need. In other words, I am encouraging you to think more deeply and subtly about what you are doing when you give healing: Does this person need counselling? Do I need to use Karmic Healing, or Conceptional, Ancestral, Archetypal or Homoeopathic Healing? Do I need to use a combination, to work through one situation with my client using one type of healing, and then move on to another? Indeed, Homoeopathic Healing can be used and extended beyond the concepts that I have given you; it can be used for other forms of healing.

EXERCISE: Homoeopathic Healing with a client

As in every other form of healing I have talked about, you will need to be in your own state of balance, your own harmony, within your own focus and wholeness before you start and when you finish. You will not want to be the recipient of your client's condition, and if you are in balance and in harmony within yourself, then you will be contained and protected and it is unlikely that this will happen.

Place yourself within a golden circle with an equidistant cross at its centre. . Relax and attune yourself, centering and balancing within your wholeness...cleanse your auric field, either by sieving (see Chapter 4) or by imagining that you are standing beneath a crystal clear waterfall. Sense a note of inner harmony clearly resonating within you.

Now, I would like you to move into your inner senses, into your feelings, into your very being; and to allow that finer part of your consciousness to expand gently beyond the boundary of your body. Allow yourself to move into another frequency of experience, one that is finer, more gentle, but more profound. On this frequency you can take responsibility for your own spiritual seeking, you can have your own conversations with God, in the sense that you are harmonising with the God energy that is omnipresent in every part of the universe. For that finer frequency is within you as well as without.

In finding the divinity within, you are acknowledging that you can touch that God energy within your own being because you are part of it. Each one of you is capable of the self-realisation of that spiritual 'other' part of you, of sensing it and of feeling unconditional love.

Fill your whole being with God energy - feel it coming right through you, right through that finest filter within your aura. You are now poised to give healing.

At this moment, feel and hold the energy of unconditional love within your being. In your mind, consider that energy as 100% healing energy. Now allow it to condense into 1%. You will be sending out a finer potency of that healing energy; yet, in that 1% is the essence of the 100% cosmic love that you are channelling. So, it is not the normal 'whoosh' of energy; it is a very fine, delicate and focused energy. It might help you to think of it as being on a finer frequency.

Now, using your fine frequency of God energy, channel it to your client and allow it to 'touch' him/her lightly. . .it can touch the heart, it can touch the throat, it can touch the crown or the base chakra, it can touch any one of the chakras. . .As it touches the chakric points in your client you may experience a corresponding chakric resonance within your own body.

Allow this fine focus of unconditional love to create a level of harmony and balance within the whole chakric system and within the whole person, remembering that it is still a homoeopathic potency on a very sensitive energy level.

If you wish to apply this energy physically, just touch one finger of each hand on either side of the temple, or at the front and back of the head. The same could be applied in distant healing. Also, an image that might be helpful for some is to imagine that you are offering the person that fine frequency of energy as a golden homoeopathic pill.

When you have finished, realign your client strengthening their auric field, and rebalance and harmonise the energies within yourself, earthing yourself well.

To summarise: Using a laser beam of unconditional love, you touch the most sensitive level of unconditional love within your client.

With the amount of cosmic energy that is being released to the planet, you will need to think in terms of Homoeopathic Healing more frequently. You will find that when you begin to use it, it will not only be just as effective, it will be *more* effective; because the fineness and sensitivity of it will go straight to the innermost part of the person to whom you are offering healing.

Homoeopathic Healing Case Study

Carolyn, who is now 20, had hydrocephalus (water on the brain) at birth. She has autism and other medical problems that meant that she has had to undergo many operations as a young child. After these operations, Carolyn changed considerably, often taking on the mannerisms of her great grandmother – who had died previously. Two years after the operations finished, Carolyn spoke about how she experienced the anaesthetic and the link with her great grandmother. Carolyn does speak in a limited way, in short sentences repeated many times.

When she is left alone by her mother now, she becomes distressed to the point of being physically sick, she becomes violent and has to be strongly restrained. She is about to be placed in a residential unit for adults with autism. Her father left when she was very small and her mother is in a new relationship which Carolyn finds very difficult. She has been diagnosed as autistic, agoraphobic, having ADHD (Attention Deficit Hyperactivity Disorder), and she has also had a seizure disorder. Her mother speaks of the years of outbursts and aggression – there are holes in the wall to prove it. Carolyn loves music of all kinds and she practises relaxation and meditation.

The first four distant healing sessions (Caroline lives in America) were focussed on bring her into balance, clearing and delinking her from negative energies, grounding and strengthening her whole system. The most important aspect of this was strengthening the links between the chakras. At this stage, I was using healing energy in the normal way as it felt important for Caroline to be prepared energetically, so that she could utilise Homoeopathic Healing in the best possible way.

On the fifth session, I felt that Homoeopathic Healing was now the most appropriate form of healing for her. I sent the fine potency and then gave her a 'homoeopathic golden pill' as mentioned by H-A. Her whole system opened up and her chakras began moving in a very beautiful way, releasing colour and light into her auric field.

I repeated the same process four days later. Again, she opened within herself - her energy was flowing freely and her whole system seemed clear, strong and balanced. At this point I received feedback from her mother and a request for the healing to be continued:

"When the healer began sending healing to Carolyn, I could not believe the change. It was almost immediate!! It is possible now to reason with her. She speaks in full sentences. She seems to understand what is happening to her body. She also deals with disappointment, which is something she never dealt with easily. Everyone in the household knew it. I feel that Carolyn is connecting mind, body and spirit. I know that she is able to distinguish things that are going on. . . . She is also more grounded. God Bless You."

69

Chapter 9

DISTANT HEALING

Distant, or remote Healing, can work because the aura of a person comes out in waves, and each wave is larger than the previous one. These resonances travel out and out and can reach right round the world. This is how Distant Healing works. Often it would be beneficial if you could meet the client at some time or be really aware of their nature and situation, because it is about finding that point of contact, that point of synchronicity that brings the healing energy and the client together. But on a purely psycho/spiritual level, remote healing can very often be successful. Obviously it will not be so easy on the mental/ emotional levels; and these play an important part in any healing because the clients need to understand the cause of their problem.

It must be stressed that healing should never be given directly to anyone without their permission. If given without their permission through a request by another person, it can be sent to surround them so that it is there for them to take if their spirit wishes to accept it. Otherwise you could be forcing them into a situation against their will.

Healing should never be given with the idea of making somebody better but with the object of enabling the spirit within to know where and how it needs healing, and what it needs to do about the healing it is being given. When that happens, then what healers call a miracle can occur. I would call it instant recognition.

It is important to bring the subject *to you*

With regard to Distant Healing generally, either to a person, a situation or a country, I would like to issue a word of caution. When using any of the healing modalities I have spoken of, including the collective Planetary Healing, it is always safer and usually more helpful for the healer to mentally bring the situation to themselves, rather than project themselves to the situation. I understand that for someone who is very sensitive, it is easy and can be very satisfying to have an out-of-body experience. But you make yourself very vulnerable in doing this and the whole criterion of Earth incarnation is to be able to experience *within* the body. And that applies to every level of experience.

When I refer, for example, to sensing and communicating with your Higher Self, I am meaning lighten your vibration to feel a finer frequency within. Bring *it* to *you*; bring *it* to your *consciousness*, do not reach up to it.

Interestingly enough, a number of years ago, this sensitive through whom I speak used to love coming out of his body to meet me. And I had to convey to him that, yes, this is a way to harmonise and link with my energy, but you are using up tremendous reserves of your own energy to do this. Allow me to come to you for, when you are out of the body, you are very much more vulnerable.

The whole fundamental basis of my teaching is about self-responsibility, self-realisation and empowerment, and when you are out of your body, you need an experienced person to look after you and protect you. Your personal guardian angel will always protect you in natural occurrences such as sleep, but not if you deliberately eject yourself out of the body as in astral projection, 'taking' yourself to the situation. The danger is that you could bring back negative energy to yourself.

So always bring an image of the person or subject into your circle, into your room, and work on it as if it were in front of you.

Sending love to overcome 'evil'
Life within a physical body holds limitations. You are limited by the physical body, the emotional capacity and the brain capacity. So when I express these concepts, I am fully aware that no spirit within a physical body is totally non-judgmental, these are ideals that we are working towards. It is only within the Godhead that unconditional love is completely possible.

It is difficult to fully understand, within the context of a human frame, that harmony can only be achieved through balance and that one needs the shadow in one's life to see the light. There is not a spirit in physical incarnation on this planet who has not had thoughts that you would conventionally believe to be undesirable - even 'evil' - such as envy, jealousy, hatred or the misuse of power.

It is important to acknowledge that and to try to understand these things as part of your love.

When you are sending thoughts of unconditional love to someone who has just mutilated a child, for instance, I understand that it can only be as far as you are able. But the fact that you are trying to come to terms with and understand it is a major step forward. It is the simplest and yet most difficult concept of all. So send out your thoughts on the highest possible level, thoughts of unconditional love, forgiveness and respect.

Editor's note: When giving healing under these circumstances, you may find it helpful to use the following visualisation:

Holding the Mandorla

"It is not that the light element alone does the healing;
the place where light and dark begin to touch is where
miracles arise . . . that is where God is." Robert A. Johnson

The Mandorla
This meditation is for healing the opposites in ourselves, the para-doxes that we find difficult to reconcile, or for extending as distant healing to another person or situation. It is based on a Mandorla, the almond shape created when two circles overlap.

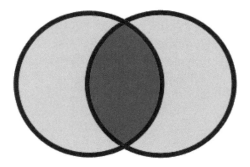

This is the place in which we can hold and integrate two opposite qualities we see in ourselves, for that is where healing takes place: such qualities as openness and scepticism; dominance and sub-servience; love and hate; light and shadow; or tolerance and intolerance. In other words, any two attitudes or parts of oneself which are paradoxical. We all have them, if we look deep enough.

Visualisation
Prepare yourself by finding a place of inner stillness. . . Then hold in your awareness the two opposite qualities you wish to work with. . . Place your hands, palms upwards, on either side of your body, on the same level and a little away from it . . . Each hand has a large sphere sitting on it, and each sphere contains one of the opposite qualities you have chosen to work with. . . . Focus strongly, one at a time, on the contents of the two spheres, feeling quite distinctly the separate qualities contained within them, with neither judgement nor partiality. They are both aspects of yourself.

Very slowly move your hands towards each other until the two spheres touch and overlap, creating a large almond shape in the middle. Move into that almond shape in your imagination and be aware of the paradox. Feel the intermingling of these two opposites as they blend within your being.

In that state of integration, say to yourself:

"I am the totality of all aspects of myself. I am what I am, no more, no less. I am a whole being."

When this simple exercise feels complete, gently allow the imagery to fade as you gradually become conscious again of your whole self and every part of your body, still retaining the feeling of integration you have generated in your whole being. . . Centre and ground yourself.

Chapter 10

INTRUSIONS
FROM BEYOND THE SELF

Introducing Mental Healing

Different Types of Healers

This brings us to the subject of healing the mind, which is a more complex and somewhat broader field of work for we are dealing not only with the physical body and the aura but also with outside influences. No person should be engaged in mental healing unless he has been specially instructed in it, for if this advice is ignored there could be a danger to the healer's own mental balance.

The power of the human mind is very great, as psychologists of today are rapidly learning. Many diseases of the human body, physical as well as mental, are psychosomatic, originating from the mind. Thus, physical and mental healers will often work together on one case, for it is necessary to cure the cause before the effect can be tackled successfully.

When confronted with a case of mental maladjustment the healer must first ascertain the cause. These may be many and varied. The most common ones are:

(a)   When the spirit within the body is young or weak and is easily influenced by those around, both in life and from the spirit world. In such a case the spirit will pay more attention to an interfering influence than to the task of controlling its own physical body, and this causes great confusion of mind to the person concerned.

(b)   Cases of possession, ranging from the violent elemental type to the more subtle possession by a spirit from a higher plane.

(c)   Cases of attachment in which an earthbound has attached itself, because of past associations, with the host or its own parasitic agenda.

Let us start with the former. We can assist a weak native spirit by bringing it closer in to the physical body. This one does by strengthening both the cords where they connect the spirit to the body, at the head and the solar plexus, so that spirit and body can work together in greater harmony away from distracting influences. The spirit will then be able to assume greater control of its body. It is rather like the puppeteer who controls the puppet by pulling strings. If one of those strings snaps then that portion of the puppet to which it is attached will cease to function correctly. If, however, he refastens the string the limb will again respond to his will.

There are no intermediaries in Mental Healing, no guides, spirits or deceased doctors that take possession of the healers and do their work for them. All is carried out in conscious command, for this is the age of reason when man must learn that to lean on the discarnate when he is in fact capable of doing the job himself is helping neither them nor him.

It has been found from experience that healers fall into certain groups or categories according to their own individual make-up and the way in which they act as channels for the cosmic forces. According to the type of ray produced by the mind of the healer, so will he or she be equipped to deal with, say, a physical case, a psychological case, or a patient who is disturbed mentally.

For a mentally disturbed case, a yang healer with a strong outgoing flow of energy is better equipped to clear any attachment or possession, which may have intruded because of the patient's mental and auric lack of balance, and to send it on its way. A yin healer, being very receptive, could unwittingly draw an entity to themselves and would then also need clearing by the yang healer. This is the way exorcisms were carried out in the past, but it can be dangerous and I would not recommend it. Such healing is best carried out by two specially trained yang healers, unless a yin healer is experienced in yang procedures and can summon a strong yang energy.

The Relationship between the Body and the Spirit

The human body is governed by the stage of evolution of the spirit. There can be strong links between the psychological make-up of a person and their physiological appearance. But it is the spirit that controls the human mind, for the brain is but a computer and, without the spark of spirit to programme it, it would be no more than a zombie.

The human body was designed to function under certain conditions, within a given temperature range and with balanced amounts of chemicals in its system. Should there be a sudden alteration in any of these conditions the spirit will be forcibly ejected from the body, causing the person to faint, enter a coma or even die.

Let us take alcohol as an example. The human system has an average alcoholic content and if this is added to, slowly the body can acquire a limited tolerance. Some people are unable to acquire this tolerance and their bodies reject the excess soon after it is taken in. This is the result of a certain defence mechanism triggered off by the spirit as a protection against physical poisoning or loss of conscious control. However, many people do not have this ability and when any excess of alcohol is retained in the body the chemical imbalance becomes accentuated and the symptoms of drunkenness will result. If the excessive intake is repeated too often the body becomes slowly poisoned. One of the symptoms of drunkenness is insensibility, or lack of control of the spirit over the body; the misalignment caused by this condition weakens the aura and can attract entities which may attach themselves - a condition not to be desired.

This rejection of the body by the spirit will also occur if the temperature of the body is changed to any degree, for the spirit or ego will only retain control under set physical conditions. Drugs act in much the same way, forcing the spirit from the body; the inhalation of certain gases which cause an unnatural imbalance in the chemical make-up of the body, has a similar effect.

Care should be taken when a person is in a state of artificially induced unconsciousness that alien entities are not allowed to take over the cords controlling the body (these are the silver cords connecting the spirit to the physical body at the head and the solar plexus) and cause a possession. It occasionally happens that a person 'never seems the same' after, say, an operation when his spirit has been forcibly ejected by the use of anaesthetics. In the treatment of mental cases shock treatment is sometimes employed; this will serve to eject the possessing spirit for a short period but unless the aura is sealed properly afterwards, it may well return, as the native spirit without assistance from a healer, might find the task too difficult.

Physical and mental deformity

Finally, we come to the question of such cases as Down's syndrome and backward children. Fuller details are given to healers who specialise in this type of healing but, briefly, such conditions are usually due to:

(a) lack of alignment between the physical and etheric bodies so that the spirit cannot influence the physical brain to assume control of the nervous system of the affected parts;

(b) the entrance into a human body of a spirit that is not in a suitable state of evolution for human existence;

(c) a karmic condition personal to that spirit.

Diagnosis

As for diagnosis, legally, the layman is precluded from making a medical diagnosis, which is indeed a good thing. So, in observance of the law, energy healers do not make a point of telling their patients what they feel is wrong. However, by the use of that extra sense, call it etheric sight or the third eye as you will, the healer is often able to understand intuitively the primary cause of the trouble, and offer a few tentative suggestions that could help the patient to rid himself of his trouble in the ordinary course of life. The advice might be for more rest, a regulated diet, or even an immediate visit to a physician; but no more. The healer needs to be prepared to listen to any problems and discuss possible solutions.

It is possible to bring about miracle cures but great power would have to pass through the healer and the amount of power any healer can take at one particular time is dependent upon many factors. The physical body needs to be trained to take a high vibration and few people today are prepared to put themselves out sufficiently to achieve the necessary balance between spirit and body to take such power.

Since Advanced Energy Healing is carried out by the power of thought, time and space are no barriers and a considerable amount of Distant Healing can be undertaken. While some healers find they are able to concentrate more easily on a patient who is present, others find that by picturing the sufferer mentally or tuning into their vibration they are able to achieve an equal amount of concentration.

Although we speak of a 'healer' who 'cures' a sufferer, what the healer is actually doing is assisting the patient to cure himself. A healer is a person who is a suitable channel for a certain type of power which, when directed by thought to the etheric body of a sufferer, aids the patient's own spirit to make the necessary adjustment.

The healing ray is a double-edged sword that energy healers are trusted not to misuse for they need to understand the karmic rebound this would cause. Neither is it to be used for entertainment purposes but solely for the benefit of mankind.

Past Life Regression & Self-Healing

Past life healing is of vital importance but at the outset I would like to make it clear that it needs to be done only after proper training and guidance. Also, it cannot be imposed. It has to be carried out with the willingness of the person to go back into a past life situation in a way that is devoid of ego. So many people like to romance about past lives, to feel that they may have been Nefertiti, Mary Magdalene, Jesus and so forth.

If a person is going to delve into past life therapy it should not be done for ego reasons. It should only be undertaken if you want to face and acknowledge some of the pain and difficulties affecting your present life which may have origins in your past. By going back into that past you can begin to see it, confront it, acknowledge it and allow yourself to move beyond the need of whatever it was.

So much depends on the motive. You have to allow it to happen, and you must not try to influence it with your own fears. In other words, when a person goes into a past life situation it is very easy for them to sabotage themselves. It is not so much the detail of the life that is important but the nature and the relevant energies of the obstruction.

You must remember that God does not judge. God is a God of unconditional love, forgiveness and respect. We are at a time in the history of this planet when it is important for people to be free to enter tomorrow without being shackled to the past. Even some of what I have said in this book may be out of date by the time you read it. What is needed now depends on how you move and release yourself from the past and thereby open yourself to new dimensions of understanding.

Past life regression should only ever be done in a way that allows the person to find out which life it is, where it is and what they experienced that is relevant to this life. If a therapist tells them, 'This is what you were in your past life and this is what you should be doing', they are doing great harm to that person and that spirit. Such people must be properly trained and have spiritual under-standing.

Past Life Self-Healing

The following is the kind of group regression procedure that I have used. First, of course, all the participants need to be taken through the relevant preparation for healing as presented earlier.

Now, I am going to ask you to recall a situation that you feel deep down inside you is very unresolved. . . . sense that feeling in your body, it may have a colour, it may have a shape . . . Allow that feeling to take you back into a relevant past life situation . . . allow yourself to experience a situation in which there is something unresolved . . . Say to yourself:

"I own within me that this feeling relates to this past life and perhaps other past lives; and at this point in time I feel ready to release and let go of those lives - to acknowledge that there is part of me that knows that this feeling has been with me for a long, long time. I have allowed it to stay there, knowing that at some time I would have to face it and deal with it."

This can be a very painful process because in many cases it will involve you going back into a situation in which there was a great deal of pain, a great deal of suffering, and often a great deal of injustice:

"Why was I treated like this? Why was I subjected to this fear, the constant being put down, trodden on, my emotions and feelings being squashed? Is the shadow going to be there with me for eternity? Can I ever really move beyond it?"

Now that, interestingly, is your choice, there are no ifs, shoulds or buts, it is your choice. But one thing you can do is to acknowledge that that past life experience which is still giving you this feeling of insecurity, of being out of control, can be placed into a rightful perspective. So I want you to look at both the light and shadow of this feeling and say:

"Yes, I did suffer. Have I learnt from it? What have I learnt? How have I grown from it? What has it given me the determination to do in this life or in a future life? To help others? To prevent others being put into such a situation? To learn and understand that unconditional love is the only ultimate answer?"

I would like you to say out loud the following words:

"I love myself for what I am. I acknowledge what I might have been. I honour what I might have learned from it. Am I ready to move beyond it? I am going to try. . . (louder) I release the negativity of that past life experience. . . I allow myself to move beyond it with great joy. . . And this new dimension of energy that I am drawing on within me is lifting me above the need of criticism and judgment of myself and of others. . ."

Now, breathe deeply in and out three times, each time feeling that you are releasing and letting go of that burden . . . and I think you will find a new energy entering your total being on all four levels. Allow yourself to reach out, to lift your arms, to open your heart, to open your mind, to open your whole being. . . . and, as I say this, I would like you to try and think and feel it in every cell of your being. Express the following:

"I have come into this incarnation to experience, in a new open way, in which I have released myself from a deep level of unnecessary burden. I acknowledge that I am a beautiful creation of God, I acknowledge that I am part of God as God is part of me. . . we are one."

Now, gently return to the here and now. Acknowledge your physical body, ground yourself, feel a new person, feel that new energy, knowing that you can now face the world from yet another dimension of being, of experience. Bless you.

And now, dear friends, how does that feel? Do you feel lighter, brighter and mightier?

80

Spirit Release

Leading on from this, I would like to speak with you about Spirit Release and how Advanced Energy Healing and, particularly, Homoeopathic Healing, can be used in a broader way to help individual spirits stuck in a group situation. In this I am referring to the release of spirit when it becomes locked out of time, when it cannot see how to move forward and how to release itself from the karmic situation in which it has become entangled.

How does such a situation take place? It can happen in a number of ways. It can happen through a violent form of death as in a war or as in Hiroshima when the nuclear bomb was exploded. It can happen when the person dies and the spirit is locked into unreleased anger and resentment. It can also happen when, during its life the spirit has been unable to communicate properly with its soul and mind, its heart and its body and, as a result of this, it has become caught in a kind of timeless vacuum.

This can happen if the circumstances around that spirit during a lifetime embody a group energy that prevents it from being able to express itself, in the sense that it is completely restricted by the tenets of a very strict philosophy or religion.

Ancient Egyptian Stuck Energy

A very good example of this happened in Ancient Egypt, where the structure of that religion became very politically motivated and status conscious. After the downfall and sinking of Atlantis, many Atlantean spirits reincarnated into the Egyptian civilisation. They were determined not to fall into the traps that they had lived through in Atlantis – traps of escalating negative energy to such a degree that they lost sight of their own spiritual heritage, their understanding of God, and finally destroyed themselves and their continent.

Those spirits had built a very tight philosophy in Egypt, a very tight religion, and became overly detailed in the way in which a spirit reincarnated. You reincarnate, they said, into the same status, into the same position in life. Over the years more and more Egyptian spirits became stuck; the positions were not there to reincarnate into. They even wanted to reincarnate into the same sex. So the Egyptians created a framework of stagnation. And, in my opinion, the stuckness of those Egyptian spirits is contributing to a lot of the difficulties in the Middle East today.

Any religion that uses dogma is creating an energy that controls and many of your religions have been based on fear, guilt and what would happen if you do not toe the line. When there is such a strong hold on the spirit through powerful beliefs embodied into the energetics of a religion, it prevents a spirit from moving forward because it short circuits the energy or frequency on which that spirit operates. Indeed, some very strict religions and beliefs on your planet at this moment in time can actually create locked karma.

For example, if a religion is based on power and fear and teaches that there is an afterlife but does not allow for the concept of reincarnation, what happens when the person dies and the spirit moves on? Sometimes a spirit is able to adjust itself, but sometimes it becomes locked into the very tenets of that religion. This can happen especially if it is a young spirit that does not have the weight of karma and experience behind it to enable it to move forward, to look back over its life and evaluate it in a free way.

As an incarnate person, the more you can blend the spirit with the body and blend the body with the spirit, the more you are able to understand where you are, how you are and what you are. You also begin to savour and to experience unconditional love, through which you can learn how to forgive. All these states of being are not just about adjusting a psychological viewpoint or dealing with an emotional blockage, they are actually to do with that synthesis of spirit, mind and body, bringing you together as a whole.

One of the reasons I am speaking about Spirit Release is that I see it as another form of healing that needs to be taken in great depth as we move forward into this 21st century. Because whilst this may not seem to affect you directly, it is having a very power-ful influence indirectly. Around the planet over the thousands of years that it has been inhabited by homo sapiens, there has been a tremendous amount of stuck energy accumulating.

A 'Fog' Descends

The Ancient Egyptian energies were very strong and still are; so strong that they have created a blanket of mist over the Middle East that affects not only Egypt, but also Iran, Iraq, Israel, Palestine, Lebanon and the neighbouring countries that have suffered and are still suffering so much turmoil over the years. And much of that turmoil is being fed by the blanket of fog which surrounds these countries. It is stifling, forcing them inwards.

Approximately 2000 years ago, Jesus the man took on the Christ energy; and part of what he took on was actually the commencement of a spiritual strategy to try to lift this fog. But despite the very beautiful energy surrounding Jesus, the fog fed the negativity and brought out the shadow. When it is a very heavy day and there is a thick fog, everything comes down, does it not? And although this 'fog' that I am referring to is not visible to the human eye, it is like a thick fog of energy that absorbs other energy; but it absorbs it in such a way that it does not return it.

Cosmic energy or spirit energy is like electrical energy. Can you imagine a situation whereby you are feeding electricity into something and nothing happens, it is just absorbed? The energy that is absorbed actually increases the thickness of that fog and this has gone on for thousands of years. There is so much beauty, so much potential in that Middle Eastern part of the world, that if the fog can be released, it can bring about a spiritual renaissance in that area. Not a spiritual renaissance that is built of fear, but a spiritual renaissance that is built on love.

Indirectly, this fog has affected not only the Middle East, but also religions that have been created in that area. You have, for example, the Christian religion: it is being affected by that fog so that much of the love that the religion is trying to send out is being absorbed and not returned. But love needs to circulate, to be given and received, so this fog creates within that religion a kind of desperation; it creates an intolerance, it creates a rigidity, a blindness, because it cannot see through the fog and is stuck where it is.

Now, I want to make it very clear that this is not an attack on any one religion, for I honour and respect all religions on the planet. Within each one there is a dedication and a need to enlighten humanity. But I am aware that they are having to face a battle which is unfair. They are having to face, I believe your earthly expression is 'odds', odds that are unfair.

Another instance of what can happen is as in the fate of the Cathar religion in the South of France where thousands of people were put to death under the most appalling torture. This created another fog because those spirits died in such a way that they could not see where they were, or what they were. Some will have moved on but others became entrapped.

Words of warning:

Spirit Release is a branch of healing to be used *only* by experienced healers in a group. For if you are not experienced in using a strong, outward, 'yang' flow of healing energy under adequate protection, you could draw negativity back to yourself from a negative situation.

If you decide to tackle something like this, *tune in to just one spirit at a time* and try to help it, making sure that you work within a strong protection.

Do not attempt anything that you do not feel ready to touch. Only deal with what you intuitively know you can handle. The techniques I suggest need to be assessed in the light of where you are, what type of Spirit Release you wish to tackle, whether it is a spirit that has become stuck because of an accident or whether you are facing thousands of lost souls. If you wish to spend part of your life doing Spirit Release work, then make your choice clearly and you will find that circumstances will present themselves to you.

If you are one of a group wishing to send Homoeopathic healing to, for instance, spirits from Ancient Egypt held in a static fog, each member of the group needs to send healing to one spirit that they individually feel drawn to. Even one spirit released will subtly lighten the fog and encourage others to shift their mental stuckness. *Note:* At least one person from the group needs to maintain a strong protection round all the healers.

HEALING EXERCISE: Spirit Release after a traumatic group death or a static 'fog' from the past

Think for a moment of individual spirits from a serious railway or aeroplane accident where many lives have been lost. What emotions do you think would have been experienced by the victims, extreme pain. . . terror. . . anger? Perhaps they would have questioned why it had happened to them. Why they had been in that particular place at that time? Maybe they would have felt enormous confusion about what had actually happened and a sense of disorientation. The relatives, and many other people who were affected indirectly, would also have experienced similar emotions. And if you put all these feelings together, they would also create a kind of fog, a fog of confusion that can remain for generations.

Prepare yourselves individually and as a group for Homoeo-pathic Healing (see chapter 8) with at least one person holding a protection around all. Each healer then centres their thoughts on just one of those souls who died, whoever they may be, and surrounds them with that fine, delicate homoeopathic love energy. As I mentioned in the earlier exercise, you may find it helpful to imagine that you are offering the healing, the fine frequency, as a golden homoeopathic pill. You will need to talk in your mind to the spirit to whom you are offering healing, explaining what has happened. Speak to it on the following lines:

"You can and you are able, if you so wish, to move on. For, in moving on, you can help others. Stay where you are and you will be there for a long time. If you feel ready to move on, use my healing energy as a crutch to lift yourself above the fog. If you do not feel ready now, hold that energy, hold the crutch that I am offering you; then when you do feel ready, move forward and lift yourself above the fog. . . Lighten yourself. .   . . Lighten yourself! . . .and go forward on your evolutionary path. . ."

Bring yourself back to everyday consciousness, ground yourself well and feel centred within your auric field.

If, in your healing, you enable one of those spirits to start to feel and experience in that way, you are beginning to bring light into that fog. You are beginning to relieve that burden and release that spirit. Perhaps it will have an opportunity to ask questions in another lifetime, or to help in a future similar situation.

However, I would warn all healers never to *force* a stuck spirit to move on. That type of Spirit Release is very dangerous, as it creates the very situation you are trying to avoid. You cannot banish a spirit; that is only punishing it. You can only enable it to rise above the need of the stuckness in which it is incarcerated. Explain to it that you are there as a support, not to manipulate; and as you begin to create movement in the fog, the whole situation will move forward. It will be easier to help the next one because the first will have made a path and opened up the way.

Reminders:
If you work with energies that have been imprisoned for thousands of years, such as the Egyptian, I would advise you to do so only in a group situation in which you are being adequately protected.

On no account use manipulation and if you use Homoeopathic Healing, work with only one spirit at a time. It needs a non-manipulative approach and a great deal of love and support.

If you are working within a group, with protection, maybe you will feel ready to work with more than one spirit in a session. But one at a time. The whole key is to build slowly and move forward only when you are ready to take the next step.

Spirit Attachment*

The need for Mediums to protect themselves
When a person is a natural sensitive - that is, mediumistic – they are not always aware of the fact. Many cases of schizophrenia, hallucination and so-called vivid imagination, are simply those sensitives who walk through life with open auras through which penetrate all sorts of other spirit minds. They can even be possessed for periods when they are 'not quite themselves' without the possessor being necessarily of a malevolent nature. It may be a spirit from the second plane that wishes to communicate something which it has learnt, or a spirit that died in a very sudden way and wishes to come straight back into a body, or maybe one that wishes to send a message to a loved one.

When a person is receptive he is not only receptive to good influences but to all influences; hence the cases of brilliant artists and composers who receive much of their inspiration from the 'other side' but whose private lives are often far from inspiring. A good and well-trained sensitive will learn to keep his or her aura closed at all times, except when he is working and fully protected.

The Weakness of the Young Spirit

We need to look now at cases of a person with a very weak nature who is not just influenced by spirit entities, but where a spirit other than the native or host spirit starts to interfere with that person's body. Spirit attachment is, very simply, just that. The invading entity may just latch itself on to a person's aura and draw off some of the energy. It may actually enter the aura and be inside the body together with the native spirit, which can often result in what you call schizophrenia. It can also reject the native spirit and take over the body entirely.

Specially trained people must be called in to deal with this. Cases of possession by malevolent or degraded spirits exhibit lunacy, sex-mania, the tendency to commit crimes, fits and violent changes of personality. The possessing spirit must be sent to its own sphere of evolution. When a person has been subjected to the strain of being controlled by an alien entity it will take time to build up both the physical body and the aura after the correct spiritual adjustment has been made. A post-possession case must be watched very carefully and recharged regularly until the native spirit has regained complete control of its mind and body.

Sadism and sado-masochism are but two of a series of aberrations that occur when a young spirit takes on a physical body with a clever brain. The spirit has neither the wisdom nor experience to control and channel the mental energies into creative fields, so it seeks outlets in perverse physical expression. People of this nature attract lower entities of their own order and if they are not careful a spiral of degradation can ensue. They can best be helped by joining a disciplined and ethically well-organised group or section of society and, of course, if they should attract discarnate intelligences of a low order, an experienced mental healer would be required to heal the situation.

These things happen a great deal, particularly where there has been drug misuse and in traumatic situations, for when there is an accident or a deep trauma and the native spirit is in a state of shock for a time, it can lose control of the body. And if the protecting energy - the auric field - is not in balance because of the negative state of mind of that person, it can easily draw negative energy in the form of an unbalanced spirit towards it. A spirit that attaches itself in this way is usually angry or damaged.

The attachment can be drawn from another person; or it can be a spirit earthbound in an area where there has been a lot of tragedy and many people have been killed unfairly or unjustly. This can happen in places like prisons where death sentences are carried out, for this can draw angry spirits, particularly if someone is put to death who is innocent. And I can assure you that many people who are put to death in the name of justice are innocent, or they have not been understood, or they have not been helped; so they die bitter, angry, and resentful, hating the society which has condemned them.

Such a spirit may move on; but it may stay around and look for those whom it feels condemned it. It may attach itself to someone's aura to try and bring on a disease that is particularly agonising and cause immense pain and distress, for it is looking to re-create what it feels has happened to it.

Oh, when humankind kills in the name of justice, little does it realise the dreadful karma that it creates for the spirit of the person who is killed!

There will be the rare occasion when the spirit feels that it was just that it should die in this way, but in the majority of cases it will carry anger and hatred towards the society that caused it.

Spirits who Choose to Reject God

Then we have to include those who reject God, as distinct from those who simply do not believe in God. A spirit may reject God at any moment in its evolution because it has free will. In doing so, it may pander to its fears, and it may look for personal power and control over others. But when that power and control over others is exercised to the extent that the spirit completely rejects God, it can only exist by drawing on the energies of other spirits. And it will draw towards it negative energies, 'evil spirits' some may call them. 'Negative energies' is the term that I prefer.

So the spirit that has rejected God can itself become possessed, drawing other spirits towards it that are too weak to resist. Then instead of being just one spirit, there will be a conglomeration of negative energies. This is a form of self-induced spirit attachment and can be seen in evidence on a physical level in any organisation that is creating and pandering to the ego, looking for personal power, offering energies far beyond its ability to deliver.

Abuse, Trauma, Depression.

Trauma is a big cause of spirit attachment, especially when a child is abused by parents or by an institution, or by the state. Because when a spirit enters a body it doesn't mature into the body until the person is twenty-one, so during those twenty-one years there is a vulnerability - and it needs to be understood. The wise spirit will be able to say, 'Yes, I had a traumatic childhood but it has enabled me to understand what it is like to be in that situation, therefore I have much to give to others in a similar state.'

What happens in times of trauma is, of course, dependent on the state of the person at that time. If there is extreme stress present, or the taking of drugs or alcohol occurring along with the physical and sexual abuse, spirit attachment is more likely. The depletion that usually comes with this can cause degenerative diseases; it can cause chronic depression which in itself will lead to further negative conditions such as neurosis, psychosis and allied troubles, breakdowns and all psychosomatic ailments. Severe imbalance in the way that you live and a failure to deal with your own shadow are also ways that can bring about spirit attachment. An unbalanced auric field can also occur through the body's ingestion of highly chemicalised food.

Releasing the Spirit

Spirit attachment needs a very special kind of healing. No spirit has the right to control another spirit, incarnate or discarnate, especially if the host does not wish it to be there. So, you have a right to move that attaching spirit on and away from the person it is holding onto; but it must be done without malice, it must be done without judgment. It must be done in the sense of helping that spirit into the light by offering it not punishment, not imprisonment, not torture, but an understanding in which it can realise that it does have choice.

So, not only are you moving it away from the person to whom it is attached, but you are actually offering it the opportunity to choose to move out of the state that it is in. Sometimes you will be successful, but even if you are not successful in that particular healing, at least you have given it the opportunity - and that is what matters.

I always advise that healings of this nature should be done by two people. However, it is not the remit here to go into details of the process, special training is required. But I need to emphasise that there is a great difference between spirit stuckness and spirit attachment, and when you give the healing you must have a certainty within you, which it is. It could be that the person's own spirit is in a stuck state and needs releasing. Or it could be that another spirit is linking on – attaching itself - and drawing from the incarnate person, in some cases even ousting the native spirit and living through them. If it is the latter case, it can usually be evidenced by feeling another spirit energy with the person. There are so many different ways in which it can happen.

Rescue Work

Another type of timeless vacuum is created when a spirit becomes earthbound because it does not know that its physical body is dead, or maybe it is so consumed by the anger, the hatred and the bitterness of that lifetime that it does not want to move on, it wants to stay within that negative energy. Sometimes this is what has happened when a ghost is seen walking aimlessly up and down. It follows the same path, unable to see, unable to move out of the state of thought in which it has become trapped.

This can also happen when there is a fatal accident in a train, an aircraft, a car or any form of death that is very traumatic, where the physical body is suddenly disintegrated and the whole harmony of that existence is obliterated in a second. Something as violent as a nuclear bomb can even shatter the spirit into a space of total nothingness, where it is not only unable to move on, but is also unable to comprehend what has happened; and it can take a long time for recovery to take place.

It is necessary to be properly trained to do this kind of healing service and there are many mediumistic healing groups that specialise in this work.

*For further information on releasing attached spirits, we suggest you contact the Spirit Release Foundation. Details at the end of the book.

Chapter 11

ARCHETYPAL HEALING

If you can believe that your truth is your truth and that another's truth is their truth and that there is room for both points of view, then you can go forward.

Defining the Archetypes

The sense in which I am using the term 'archetypal' is to describe a collective energy formed by shared beliefs or shared purpose, each archetype being individual and not to be compared with any other. Every civilisation represents an archetype, as does every religion. The essence of your country and its inhabitants – their character-istics, beliefs and customs - represents an archetypal energy. What is important about this is for you to be able to identify and acknowledge the archetype(s) with which you feel most associated, maybe going way back into the past.

As an example, I have in some of my lectures referred to Atlantis and the Atlantean archetype because many people today are carrying that archetypal energy. I shall enlarge on this later, but I would not want the emphasis taken out of context, and I have used it simply as an example of an archetypal lineage.

Archetypes tend to create rigid and inflexible concepts and thinking, and this in itself can create many problems. So one of the reasons why I have spoken of the necessity of acknowledging your archetypal background and if you wish - but only if you wish - moving beyond it, is for you not to feel trapped by the beliefs of any particular approach. It is when a particular archetypal energy exerts an undue influence on the overall development of an individual, against the wishes of his or her spirit, that healing becomes necessary. All too often the negative, fearful aspects of this type of archetype hold people in a bind which causes them to create sectarianism and religious fervour.

It is urgent for your planet to move forward into a much more expansive, tolerant way of thinking; for whilst in one sense everyone's truth is a truth, everyone else's truth is also a truth.

Speaking from a level of energy which lies far beyond your planet, beyond isolated belief systems, I communicate from a dimension in which the energy has moved beyond any particular archetype.

Each one of you is part of an original archetypal 'family' and within that archetype there is a given energy. Let us look at some of those archetypes. Going back into the distant past there was the Lemurian, the Atlantean, the Chinese or Indian, Shamanic, American Indian, perhaps ancient Egyptian, Greek, or maybe Judaic or Christian, Islamic, Buddhic, etc. All these archetypes have a very different 'feel' and, deep within, you will know which of them you have a strong affinity with. Any spirit that has incarnated many times will probably feel a familiarity with more than one of the major civilisations and/or religions, but there will be one basic, original archetypal family of which you are a part.

There are, of course, archetypes of smaller influence that work within a more extensive dominant archetype. You could say that a strong personal family group or clan creates an archetype. This could be a situation where a spirit reincarnates into its own family line because the pull or the purpose of that family is so dominating.

When your spirit made its choice of a particular lifetime, prior to incarnating, it will have received guidance. Most likely this would have come from the essence or flavour of the archetype to which you most significantly belong. So if your basic archetype is Atlantean, you would be bringing with you the archetypal energy of that particular approach and the unresolved issues of that civilisation.

I am using Atlantis as an example because today many of the misconceived attitudes of that civilisation are re-appearing. So I would like to consider that archetype in more detail.

The Atlantean Archetype

The Atlantean archetype is not solely of this planet; it came originally from the star, Sirius, and it came with an influx of spirits incarnating from that star. For a heavenly body evolves like a person, with different energies coming in at different times, producing further richness, creativity and understanding.

During the early part of Earth's history many fears and insecurities were generated due to incomplete transitions from one era to the next. This created energy that fuelled the negative side of the planet and all therein and thereon; and it is originally what caused the Luciferian shadow aspect of the planetary guidance to become supreme and to become the dominating energy around Earth. The shadow side manifests as fear, guilt, crime and punishment, extreme negative emotions that want to hurt and destroy.

The Atlantean influence was an early attempt to bring a more advanced sentient humanoid life to planet Earth to raise the energy after the transition from the Lemurian civilisation. The Atlantean civilisation opened itself up spiritually, and I use 'spiritual' in a narrow sense. What it did not do was keep its feet firmly on the ground and recognise that holistic spirituality is about the whole being, not one specific aspect of it

Gradually, spiritual practises became distorted and misused and the Atlantean civilisation became narrow in its approach. It was unable to balance and harmonise itself and lost the ability to stay grounded. It became too obsessive in its accomplishments and lost sight of its spiritual motivation. It became obsessed with crystal healing, obsessed with sound and obsessed with what it was going to do for the planet. But it failed to consider the real needs of its civilisation and its relationship to the entire planet; for in any process of evolution one is never alone, one is always part of a whole.

The Atlantean civilisation reached such a low point that it eventually chose to scuttle itself. It had allowed the shadow to influence it to such an extent that it destroyed the continent, literally sinking it beneath the sea. Such an act of destruction empowered the shadow, for the shadow exists on energy generated solely by negative forces. It is the supreme rejection of God energy.

Present day challenges for Humanity
In the present day transition from the Age of Pisces to the Age of Aquarius there is a great opportunity for transformation; and additional help has been brought from other parts of the universe to try to establish a balance. *But this can only be achieved by moving beyond the need of manipulation and judgement.* In other terms, you could say that the Michaelian qualities of Light need to balance and

contain the Luciferian qualities of the Shadow. And this can only be sustained by the continuing efforts of all spirits on Earth who wish to see the planet evolve in love and balance.

Present day issues for individual spirits

There are many Atlantean spirits incarnate at this time because there is a tremendous sense of wanting to redeem what they feel they have lost and the pain they feel they may have caused the planet in the past. But redemption can be dangerous if it is not understood.

True redemption is not putting right what you consider to be wrong. It is about rising above the need of your own pain and the pain of your particular group consciousness or archetype. It is a kind of spiritual forgiveness.

I have stressed very strongly and very deliberately, the need for wholeness, the need for balancing the light and the shadow, the need to move beyond polarisation. The answer is always to rise above.

Identifying your archetypal background

When you are sending distant healing in a group situation, the need for identifying the archetype of your patient(s) is less important. But on a personal level, it would be helpful for you to be aware of your own archetypal background. If you are not sure, you could ask questions deeply within yourself and offer it up as a thought before you go to sleep: 'What archetype do I feel that I am part of? With which energy do I feel the strongest resonance?'

Deep within the psyche of every incarnate spirit is an inner knowledge and recognition of his/her archetypal family and its purpose. Inner questioning and quiet contemplation will allow the energy to reveal itself.

Of course, temporary allegiance may be given to new archetypes. This is an unfolding situation and a question of harmonising the old archetypes with the new. The time is passing for isolated nations, isolated religions and isolated beliefs, because each one of those nations, religions and beliefs needs to acknowledge the others and to recognise that they are all part of each other in a global sense.

The following exercise is given for those people who, in some way, feel uncomfortable or limited by their archetypal background. Remember that working with archetypal energies, you must at all times keep yourself grounded, recognising that you are part of the planet in the here and now. You are part of wherever you live and whatever work you do. You are also part of the whole.

ARCHETYPAL HEALING EXERCISE: For yourself, your group, or to guide another.

Focus your awareness within yourself and relax . . . Feel that spiritual centre that is yourself and feel unconditional love for your whole being, including your auric field. . . Say to yourself:

"I AM WHAT I AM, NO MORE, NO LESS." See if you can be aware of an archetypal energy deep down within you - it could be one or more of many ancient or modern civilisations or religions. It could be Atlantean .. Egyptian .. Judaic .. Greek .. Christian .. Buddhic .. Muslim .. Shamanic ..or whatever. It will be different for each person . . . but try to sense the deepest one for you. For some it may be like symbolically looking into a brilliant crystal. For others it may be a deep resonance in which you feel your whole body resonating to a magical sound within; and for others a merging of many colours. For some it may be just a feeling . . . Simply acknowledge that you are part of that energy. Say to yourself,

"I acknowledge that I am part of that archetypal energy . . . . I am part of that crystal / I am part of that sound / I am part of that colour . . . I acknowledge that I am part of that energy . . . I am a unique and beautiful spirit . . . In blending myself with that energy and finding that synthesis within me, within my whole being, I can take a step forward.

"I am what I am, no more, no less. . . I have moved forward in my understanding of myself and I am ready to move beyond the support of my own past. I want to demonstrate to that archetypal energy that I can find true harmony, a true synthesis, a oneness that moves me beyond judgement, beyond manipulation, that moves me forwards and outwards. "I feel that as I uplift my own being, I am also helping to uplift my archetypal background. It involves my unconditional love and forgiveness .... it is about my

own presence and the part I am playing in the unfoldment of the planet.

"I therefore acknowledge the present and go forward in love. . . . I am lifting the barriers of judgment and releasing the past that has shackled me to myself. I forgive myself. . . . .I love myself. . . . .I release myself!.... And now I am integrating this healing shift into the DNA energy within every cell of my body."

Close down by bringing your focus back to everyday reality, grounding yourself well in your physical body .... sense your inner balance, centredness, harmony and wholeness.

Working with your own archetypal energy in this way will heighten your consciousness considerably. It will be like taking the next step forward in your growth of awareness, uplifting and intensifying contact between the innermost part of your being and the outermost part of the universe.

Each one of you has to decide within yourself where you are, what you are, how you are and where you feel an affinity. It is working within those bounds that is important for you. If you feel part of more than one archetype, then work on more than one. That is your choice. If you are approaching it with a genuine desire to achieve balance and to move beyond any stuckness, you can only help the situation. If your motivation is to find a level of acceptance, you will help yourself and, in so doing, you will help the planet. Remember that each archetype within itself is complementary to all others and each in itself is of value.

Soul Groups

It feels appropriate at this point to take a deeper look at 'soul groups' which I first mentioned in the chapter on Ancestral Healing. When a spirit is first created by God, it is created as a unique unit of energy that goes out into the universe to experience in its own unique way. It will have choice, it will have the freewill to choose its direction and the type of experiences that it needs to help it on its journey.

As it starts to evolve on planes of pre-human existence, it will become aware of other spirits experiencing in a similar way and can feel very isolated and unsure of the decisions it makes. So it will look for comfort and reassurance and will tend to create a relationship with other spirits with whom it feels an affinity. Gradually a number of spirits will come together to form what is known as a 'soul group'. The energy between them becomes collective, uniting them and yet also challenging them, because sometimes the collective will prevent the individual spirit expressing itself in the way in which it needs to. On one level you could describe the soul group as an archetype in itself and indeed the Atlantean archetype that I have mentioned is quite a large soul group. Certainly, a soul group would incarnate within a specific archetypal energy.

Now the interesting thing about spirits when they become part of a collective, is that they tend to incarnate at about the same time – and I am meaning 'time' as you understand it – say between 50 and 100 years. You will probably have experienced meeting people on a similar wavelength whom you feel you have known before. This can have an effect on other soul groups who may feel pushed out of the way in order for this particular soul group to come into incarnation; and it can cause conflict among soul groups.

This is the reason why I feel Archetypal Healing is very important, because it enables a spirit to find out where it is and acknowledge its own individuality, and to realise that it does not *have* to be part of any particular group. It is another feature of the coming Aquarian Age in which spirits will be encouraged to find their own individuality and uniqueness.

When Jesus the man was born, the spirit within that body was part of a Judaic soul group. It had decided over a number of incarnations that it needed to expand the beliefs of that time. Thus it was chosen by the Christ energy to bring in the concept of forgiveness and to overcome the need to blame. As history has shown, that spirit received an extreme reaction from its archetypal collective, hence the importance of individualising yourself in an understanding and loving way. Today, on the whole, such reaction is less prevalent, although it is still held by some religions.

So, dear friends, when you meditate, think about what you are and what you are part of. There is no right or wrong about this; but this is the time and the opportunity to move out of a rut into a new concept of understanding, if that is your wish.

Chapter 12

PLANETARY HEALING

People in the past congregated in small groups, in tribes and clans, and remnants of this can still be seen in countries such as Afghanistan with fierce tribal loyalties dividing and separating. To bring modern humanity into more integrated and accepting models of interaction is an important task of world leaders today.

At this moment in time, a tremendous amount of light is being brought to bear upon this planet. It is coming from without and from within. That light is also drawing the shadow. It is empowering Lucifer, who would like once again to be in control of Planet Earth. One of the most important factors that I would like to place before you is that this is not a confrontation. It is not Michael versus Lucifer. It is the unfoldment of the evolution and karma of Planet Earth as a whole being, a whole energy, striving to maintain its balance between light and shadow.

There have been those who have prophesied an Armageddon, and in one sense, you could say that this is an Armageddon, because it is the light coming together with the shadow. But instead of coming together in harmony, they are polarising each other and causing confrontations of disharmony, anger, rage, and hatred. When that type of negative energy is engendered, it can work in the hearts and minds of the deepest shadow within human beings, debasing them into something that wants to torture, hurt, rape. Sometimes those individuals are barely aware of what they are doing because it works on and justifies the basest part of their nature.

The world is full of factions, often in dire conflict, such as within Iraq. Countries have been splitting up, such as Ireland and the former Yugoslavia, where there is a tremendous amount of ancestral karma that has gone on for hundreds of years. The separatist movements are trying to break free in many other countries. I would not attempt to justify this type of violent behaviour but I am saying that it isn't a simple matter of putting them in their place and punishing them.

There is a method of group healing that could be applied to any country or group of people who have similar destructive patterns and stuckness; but it is really important for those who work on the path of light to understand the underlying issues. It is never one person's or one nation's fault. It is easy to demonise a particular leader, because they usually represent one of two opposing energies unable to come together in love and harmony; and if you send out thoughts of light only, you could inflame the situation even further.

Always send out thoughts of balance and harmony, of coming together, listening, respecting, communicating, understanding, illuminating, so that the conflict can be transcended. It needs to be done in such a way that it does not erupt again in another forty or fifty years' time. If it is resolved by crushing, it can only create a deeper wound that will take many generations and incarnations to heal. It needs to be healed, not condemned and punished.

It is Time to move beyond Vengeance

I realise that this is a big step for world governments to take, because most of them live within a society that demands vengeance. I believe it is only with the help of groups such as yourselves, who can see and understand the importance of balance, harmony and unconditional love, that the planet can start to be lifted out of the morass in which it finds itself.

When energy is given to a planet, it is always up to those incarnate therein and thereon, to use that energy in the best possible way. There is a great deal of shadow on the planet, and yet there is also a great deal of light. What I am trying to do is to help people move forward in a way that can take these situations above the need for this continual pulling one way or the other, like a tug of war. Let us lift the planet above the need for that repeating pattern.

When I express these concepts to you, I am fully aware that no spirit within the confines of a physical body is totally non-judgmental; I fully acknowledge that these are ideals to work towards. But I repeat that, rather than focusing mainly on 'light', I would like to suggest your healing thoughts encompass balance, harmony and unconditional love for all sides of a conflict.

Truly, there is only one stage of unconditional love in the universe, and that is within the Godhead itself. For the Godhead is a state of perfect balance between light and shadow, a state of total harmony, total balance, total understanding, total at-one-ment with all other beings or states of thought.

GROUP HEALING EXERCISE FOR A COUNTRY

In giving healing to a state or nation, you are reaching out to those people who are ready to make that move; and by enabling them to deal with their karma through a change in their attitude, they will help others by their example. This form of healing must not be a manipulation, it must not be interfering with someone else's choice and evolution. It can only work on those aspects of a person's spirit, of their psyche, to lift just that part of them that is ready to make a shift; and by so doing it can enable them to attain a balance within themselves and then move forward.

Prepare yourselves individually and as a group, within a strong protection, connecting with an angelic force, such as: Michael, Buddha, Jesus, Mohammed etc. . . Place in the centre of the group circle, a particularly troubled area and all the different ethnic cultures that make it up as a whole. . .

Having built your group energy strongly, lift the whole situation . . . lift up the anger, the bitterness, the hatred . . . lift it right up, visualising it in your own way. . . Then I want you to condense that negativity into a small seed. . . . Now, send that seed into the Sun, where it will become absorbed into the light, shadow and enlightenment of the Sun Deva, the Solar Logos, to be cleansed and ethnically balanced. Surround the whole area in a balancing symbol such as the equidistant cross in a sphere, and fill it with unconditional love, unconditional forgiveness, harmony and balance.

Close down both the group energy and your own when you have finished, thanking any universal energies you may have called on for assistance.

Combining the Modalities

In this book, I have described new healing modalities and I now want to summarise them again briefly in order to introduce my final healing modality, which uses them all in a powerful combination designed for helping national or international situations.

The first healing modality is **Karmic Healing**. This is where you are giving an individual healing, focusing particularly on healing the spirit in relation to the body; the spirit that has incarnated into that body to meet the challenges of that life, deal with them and rise above them. For every spirit has brought with it both resolved and unresolved issues. This healing focuses on the way in which the spirit relates to and communicates with the physical body, reaching out to find communion with all the different levels within the body it has chosen.

Karmic Healing incorporates chakra healing which enables the client on a subconscious level to integrate all those different levels within, so as to manifest harmoniously through the physical shell. Many diseases stem from the inability of a spirit to communicate the wisdom of its Higher Self through to the soul and thence through to the different levels of consciousness - the mind, the emotions, the body itself – all the subtle bodies that make up that person.

Then I spoke about **Conceptional Healing**. This relates to the trauma of a spirit as it enters the physical body at the moment of fertilisation of the seed. The spirit has been attracted to those parents by the energies they have radiated and they, likewise, have attracted to themselves the energy that the spirit is emanating. You, as a spirit, have to face the trauma of coming out of the freedom of the spiritual realms into the restriction of a physical body; and at the beginning of life it is a very small body. You also have to face the desires and whims of your mother; she was very important to you at that time, for she was your home, she was everything to you. But what state was your mother in when she heard that she had become pregnant? Your father, too. Were you planned, were you wanted, were you dreaded? What sort of responsibility did your parents take towards this conception?

I also explained the concept of **Ancestral Healing.** This is concerned with the genetic aspect of your life, the characteristics and qualities that your father and mother have handed down through the DNA they have received from their parents, and from all the antecedents going right back in time; and how they have dealt with all those characteristics. The ancestral gene inheritance introduces other levels of experience for the spirit in incarnation, presenting challenges which meet and add to those brought about by the spirit's own karmic pattern. This form of healing resonates backwards along the ancestral line and also extends forwards, over a minimum of seven generations.

Then there was **Homoeopathic Healing,** a way of using a fine potency of healing energy on a one-to-one basis. It can also be used in relation to Archetypal Healing. As an example, I gave the ancient Egyptian civilisation where, because of the beliefs and intent of that civilisation, spirits have become stuck and are unable to go forward and reincarnate. Interestingly enough, when this happens it actually creates a shortage of spirits ready to incarnate; and this in turn attracts many very young spirits who are not ready to take that step into physical life. They are attracted because there is a desperate need for spirits to come forward at the moment of conception. So your planet has had to face a further burden of very young spirits incarnating who find it difficult to handle the physical body. One of the suggestions I have made to deal with this type of archetypal stuckness is to use Homoeopathic Healing.

Remember, where spirit is concerned, the term 'young' does not relate to physical intelligence or how clever a person is; only to the spirit's innate wisdom. Some very clever people may have a young spirit within them and consequently, they do not have the accumulation of wisdom needed to handle that brilliant mind in the best possible way, in the wisest and most loving possible way.

As we move forward in the new millennium, the needs of the human race are drawing much heightened energies to the planet. Although what you are calling 'the new millennium' is a man-made date, nevertheless the needs of the people on the planet are drawing this heightened energy to them because of the expectation that it has created. Added to this, you have the movement from one great Solar Age into another, as I mentioned earlier, creating a very significant heightening of energy. We are finally moving into the

Age of Aquarius which relates to the gradual change of your planet's position in the solar system and is not man-made but man-observed. Being on the cusp between two great ages, when the overall influence on the planet is fundamentally changing, this also creates the effect of speeding up the vibration.

The next modality is **Archetypal Healing.** This relates to the soul group of which you are a part. Spirits tend to become part of a soul group which may relate to a religion, a sect, a country, a continent – wherever spirits come together and create group energy. There may be no problem with an archetypal energy if it is tolerant and free, or the spirit is happy with it. This type of healing is needed when dogmas and concepts are rigid and a person feels trapped in the tenets of that collective archetypal group. Major religions can create this type of situation for some spirits. So Archetypal Healing focuses on the unresolved issues of an archetypal group energy for a particular spirit or group of spirits.

Finally, we come to **Planetary Healing** which is a combination of all the other five healing modalities and must only be carried out by a group. I will guide you through it.

PLANETARY HEALING EXERCISE

For the purpose of this exercise I would like to choose Ireland as being symbolic of a national conflict that still rumbles on at this time. There are many other examples I could have chosen. You will notice that I said 'Ireland'; of course I am referring to the religious divide, in addition to the divide between the Republic of Ireland, Eire, and Northern Ireland.

We are going to do this step-by-step together, with one of you reading the following guidance out loud to the group. It is quite long and you may choose to divide it into two or three sessions.

KARMIC HEALING. First of all, relax yourselves and breathe in the healing energy of the universe . . . as you breathe out, release any doubts, any fears, any anxieties that you may have . . . In your own way connect with the unconditional love of the Godhead. . . . feel it coming down through your aura filling your whole body. . . Allow your heart to expand with unconditional love and fill your whole being . . . and then, as a group, create with your thought an auric field surrounding the whole group.

We are now going to send Karmic Healing to the collective spirits of Ireland, both Catholic and Protestant. As you feel that energy of unconditional love, I want you to move it round your group in a clockwise direction . . . round and round . . . gradually increasing in speed . . . until it rises up above the group into a spiral. As it spirals upwards it spins together into a point. And, in that spinning point is added protection, because the energy going round the group is spinning so fast that it goes forth in a way that cannot pull back any shadow.

And so the healing goes up and out, connecting across to that group energy that is Ireland, showering down as a group offering, an unconditional love offering, so that any spirit within the whole of Ireland who is receptive to it can unconsciously feel that energy. You are not forcing or manipulating anyone to receive it – it is a freewill offering of unconditional love, and that is what is important. If anyone is prepared and able to receive it, they will do so.

Having allowed that Karmic Healing energy to flow for a few moments, I want you now to come right back into full physical consciousness and to prepare yourself for sending Conceptional Healing to Ireland.

CONCEPTIONAL HEALING. For this we shall take that beautiful land of Ireland and its ambience, right back to its moment of birth, when it was first inhabited. Those spirits that came to that land created a group energy, an archetypal energy which relates to the very land itself and to the forms of evolution therein and thereon: the animal, mineral, vegetable and elemental kingdoms. What you know as Ireland was not even the same shape in those days, it was part of a larger land mass; but it was to break away to form basically what you know as Ireland today. In that trauma lies not only pain but a stuckness which has somehow, throughout history, created division.

So, with a tremendous amount of unconditional love, I want you as a group to picture the pain of that land, from the moment of its birth, as a focus of energy . . . and then to pick up the feel of that focus and place it in the centre of your circle. . . As a group, lift it above the need of that birth pain. You are lifting the whole ambience of Ireland above the need of its birth pain and all that

that has entailed. . . . Do not try to go into the details of it but tackle it as a whole. You are releasing the very beginnings of that country and lifting it above the need of that birth pain – higher and higher. . . Release! Release!! Release!!!

ANCESTRAL HEALING. Relax for a moment . . . and then breathe in deeply, drawing in cosmic healing energy again, adding your own unconditional love. Once again, send the energy round in a clockwise direction and allow it to spiral up to a point. As it goes forth to that land we call Ireland, I want you to imagine that this energy is forming a giant sieve which is sweeping right through the country, helping in a group sense to sieve out any negativity that is ready to be sieved out, this time including all the ancestral negative energy from stuck spirits going back into ancient history.

As you bring the sieve up and out at the top, you are going to send all that negative energy out into the universe to be transformed. . . . You could place it in an equidistant cross within a circle or directly into the Sun. . . Let it find its balance between light and shadow. . . Now I would like you to feel that you are giving a thought of harmony to that land and its ancestral and cultural heritage . . .You are harmonising it, giving it love, giving it a focus that will enable every spirit therein and thereon, incarnate and discarnate, to find a new clarity if they so wish.

Having sent those loving thoughts, place a very large protection around the whole land in the form of golden energy that can be there for those who are ready to be protected. If you wish to make it a golden sphere, that is fine. You could shrink the golden sphere of protection down to the size of an atom and place it in the middle of that land. Allow it gradually to expand, encompassing the whole land within it, including the spirits of all other life forms that are part of that land - the animals, vegetables and minerals, and the elemental life. This is a process that you would normally use to cleanse, harmonise, balance and protect yourself; and now as a group, you are doing it for the whole of Ireland.

HOMOEOPATHIC HEALING. Now, you are going to summon up your healing energy yet again, and then focus it down to a 1% potency. I want you to send that fine potency as a group, and feel it going round in a circle again and swirling up to a point with unconditional love. . .send it to the spirit and soul of Ireland. In doing so, you are approaching it on a level that is so fine, so subtle, a frequency that is so delicate, that it will help to loosen up any inherent stuckness anywhere in that land.

In that loosening up, I want you to understand that this is a country that in inclination is basically Christian, but representing different aspects of Christianity as a religion. Within that framework, there are spirits who have come from other archetypal energies. So in creating movement I would like you to feel that with your Homoeopathic Healing you are helping the various energies of that land to become more relaxed and forgiving and less fearful about extending unconditional love.

ARCHETYPAL HEALING. Next, we shall give the country Archetypal Healing, and for this I am going to ask you to build a golden sphere in the centre of your group and place within it the past of that country as a whole, the archetypal energy that it has created through its needs, its learning, its beliefs and its wants. You will observe that Ireland, at this time, is still very shaky ... it is not fully at peace, it is not in harmony. While the golden sphere is in the centre of the group, I would like you each to send thoughts of unconditional love and harmony to it. I am going to suggest that you do this to the count of nine ... .and then as you count from nine to twelve, lift the sphere between you - lift it up above the need of its present pain, helping it to release the stuck ways of being and thinking, the age old patterns of behaviour, resentments and suffering of the past, including those spirits of the past that are also stuck. Can you feel it floating off now? It is floating back to the land whence it came, lifting it, enabling it to become a little lighter and a little clearer.

Finally, I would like you to send out a group blessing... a blessing that will bring together all the different healing modalities you have offered to that land, so that they can work in conjunction, in harmony and at-one-ment, to release some of the burdens that those therein and thereon have had to carry. And I would like you to congratulate every spirit incarnate on that land, in whatever form, for the tremendous amount of effort, sacrifice and unconditional love that they have given to bring it to the point where it is now. Let us congratulate them for achieving the opportunities and chances that they now have, to mould themselves together once more into a land of beauty, of mystery, of character, talent and creativity.

And now come gently back into full consciousness of your body: right back into the room and centre and realign yourselves.

And with that blessing and final honouring, you have now completed what I call Planetary Healing, bringing five healing modalities together as an act of healing for a group situation. It is a form of healing that needs to be done by a group for a group in conflict; and providing that the group works within the limitation of its own understanding, it is a safe form of healing, for it is not manipulative, it is not compelling. It is an offering, as should be all healing, given with deep compassion and unconditional love and it can play a strategic part in relieving much suffering and pain during the coming years.

Global Transformation

The nature of life on Planet Earth is one of polarity. The challenge is to understand the nature of both opposing energies and to integrate them into the wholeness of our being. The outcome will be to enrich the Godhead on our eventual return, adding our unique experience to that evolving state of unconditional love and harmony.

This is a time when the whole planet and all the energies within and without are coming together and are reaching a peak in their evolutionary experience. I wish to make it very clear that the future of your planet is not predetermined, not predestined; it is the collective energy in, on and around the planet that determines the way in which it meets the various planetary initiations as they come along.

One of the difficulties that the world is experiencing is the dynamic of polarities, some of which, sadly, are religiously inspired. When it comes to global morality there is no such thing as

107

right and wrong; and there is no right standard other than that of unconditional love which needs to be sent out without reservation, without judgement, without manipulation and without any urge for an end result other than harmony and balance.

Obvious polarities at this time exist between Christianity and Islam and, on a mundane level, between the needs of corporate business and the freedom of the individual to choose. Many of these polarities are empowered by fear, the threat of insecurity, the threat of losing whatever you feel you might have gained. The only energy that can move beyond that is unconditional love. I understand and appreciate the thought energy put in by all those who would oppose war but, the stronger they become, the more they will polarise those who would support a war and therefore empower them. Again, opposing ideas need to find a balance between them.

The other difficult issue is that of trying to enable world leaders to understand that they will never find world peace by threats, by putting down, by punishment, by domination; it can only come about by listening, hearing, understanding, honouring, respecting and accepting.

It is an interesting time for this to take place because the whole ambience around your planet at the moment is for self-empowerment and the realisation of the individual. On a spiritual level, this means that every individual has access to God. No longer are intermediaries necessary.

Now, this in itself is a threat to the tribal systems on which your planet is based. It means that anyone who can accept and understand what I am saying needs to take a lead by moving beyond their own fear. And you can only do this by facing and acknowledging the fear within, and understanding that it is a part of your makeup and that without it you could not understand love. You cannot have light without shadow, nor shadow without light. You cannot have love without fear, nor fear without love. It is about bringing the two extremes together and suddenly realising that there is no need for any extreme - only for unconditional love and acceptance.

You will solve your crime problems, not by longer prison sentences, not by having more policemen; but by understanding why the crime was committed in the first place and helping those responsible to find a way through their problems and difficulties. It cannot be done by punishment. Punishment will only increase the anger, the resentment, the humiliation within that spirit. So my message to all who read this is:

> *Go forth in unconditional love, which encompasses listening, respecting and offering it up openly with no hidden agenda.*

Further thoughts on Light and Shadow

Planet Earth, as part of your solar system, is in a sense a pivot between the light and the shadow, reflecting the energies of all the other planets in the solar system. Earth's guidance also reflects the needs of every form of evolution on the planet. At the other end of the scale, the overall karma of the whole solar system is reflecting events that have taken place within the greater galaxy. And you are among the many who have chosen to incarnate when all these factors are coming into sharp focus, in order to help move the planet along.

This is why there is so much enlightenment being offered to the planet. Those higher levels of wisdom and understanding recognise that what you are having to face and deal with is not just your own karma or the karma of those around you, your family, even your past lives; but also the karma of the planet, the karma of the solar system, the karma of the galaxy. The global and the personal reflect each other.

Everything is evolving because everything is a thought of God and every thought of God is individual and unique - quite a mind-boggling concept, isn't it? But it is very important that you can see it in this outer way, so that we can focus it in an inner way.

Although you pioneers of the Age of Aquarius are doing a great job, you need to understand that you must try not to manipulate the planet. In other words, if you try to push something forward too strongly you attract the very negativity that you are trying to counteract. And this is one of the reasons why the world is in such a turbulent state at the moment.

Also, in the desire to put things right, some have closed their eyes and their minds to the fact that what happened in the past is what happened in the past, and what *needed* to happen in the past.

And so now, from the point of view of the galaxy, the solar system, the planet and yourself, the most important need is to bring all these things into a state of unconditional love and balance.

Learning from 9/11

What do you feel about the turbulence in the world at this time? How do you feel about the actions of the leaders of the United States of America? Can you relate this situation to upsets in your own personal life? It has to start with the personal.

In your private life, how do you cope with the light and the shadow? There are always two sides to any conflict. As Earth moves forward and the energy of Michael tries to contain the energy of Lucifer so as to create balance and harmony on the planet, the forces of shadow and negativity are really fighting back. Their weapons are very simple ones: fear, destructive anger, power used to disempower others, pain, guilt, suffering. What a collection of weapons!

The event that took place on 11th September in your calendar year 2001, was to change energies throughout the whole planet and, make no mistake, it created a precedent in that it suddenly opened up the whole world, creating polarities of light and darkness that were beyond any that had been created previously.

Yet I would like to say this: on a deeply subconscious level, in the American psyche the energies of violence and cruelty came to a head on 9/11 because they had sought to become more isolated in the world. They presented a polarised challenge to those shadow forces, encouraging them to strike at this power that felt above everyone else. I ask you to relate this to your own life, how you have felt at different times towards other people.

I speak not with condemnation or criticism for I understand that this is a necessary part of the evolution of every spirit to have free will to make choice. But the only way you can make that choice is to understand the shadow - and to realise that the light needs to balance the shadow. It is by bringing the light and shadow together as in a 'mandorla' (see page 72) where the two opposites meet, that the real God energy can create, uplift and enlighten.

The tragedy that took place on September 11th was not a spur of the moment operation. It had been planned for a long time. A lot of 'innocent' spirits were drawn towards it because they felt that they needed to be involved in some way, even to the extent of sacrificing their lives when they allowed the negative energies to come in and strike them; and in so doing they have fermented the situation and brought it to a head. It has offered the planet an unprecedented opportunity to rise above the need of terrorism, misunderstanding, cruel judgement and torture and the disempowerment of people.

It doesn't need me to tell you that the way through this is not through revenge or retribution. The relatives of the people who died may have felt the need to strike back. But I would ask them to open their hearts and think about it. To take revenge is what the forces of evil want you to do. They want you to play the game their way and their way is through suffering and killing and torture. You can only fight an enemy if he is there, if he won't fight you he is no longer an enemy.

It needs all sides, those who have been called terrorists, those who are in charge of governments throughout the planet. It needs them to look at the whole situation on a body, mind and spirit level. On a body level, it relates to the rich and the poor - and when I say the rich and the poor, I am including those who have food and those who do not, in other words the inequality of wealth. It also brings into the limelight the need for equality of opportunity in the human race and that includes between the sexes; neither man nor woman is superior. And if you look at the true teachings of the greatest prophets you will find that they all teach that humankind, every particle of humankind, is equal in the eyes of God.

This situation has provided an ongoing opportunity for all the leaders of the world to come together and to try to understand and deal with it on a physical level. If there is forced deprivation, whether it is through unjust rule or the unjust balance of wealth, it will create anger, resentment and hatred. And the world is reaching a point when you can no longer ignore these things.

Nature responds

You have seen a tsunami, typhoons, hurricanes and earthquakes. These are all, in a sense, planet Earth rebelling, saying, "I've had enough!" It's Gaia trying to speak out – not to destroy but to save humanity; and it is really important that you see these catastrophes as a warning to try to save you from something far worse.

111

Oh, there have been investigations and the usual cover-ups; and after the initial offers of help from world leaders, those caught up in the disasters have been woefully neglected. But underneath it all there is this energy on the planet which is saying "Humankind, wake up! The choice is yours!" The human family must, as a matter of urgency, become more conscious of Mother Earth and start a really concerted effort to halt the escalating damage to the soil and the waterways, to the plant life and the animal life and to the atmosphere which protects the planet from harmful radiation.

Natural forms of energy must have top priority over all other things because time is running out. Nuclear energy is not the answer. We are starting to see how forceful Earth can be when its beneficence is abused. This is not a message of fear and despair. No, it is not, because fear only drags you into the thing you are trying to overcome. It is a call to awaken more people to their planetary responsibilities

Heralding the new Age
The Age of Aquarius is coming, the age of consensus, the age of people finding their self-realisation, their self-responsibility, their self-empowerment. Then we move into the mind and the emotions which, of course, are what affect the physical body. How do you contact your spirit? It contacts you through your heart - but do you allow it to? Do you listen to it? Do you follow it when you know that it is the right thing for you to do?

Your spirit came into your body in this lifetime with an individual mission and a collective mission. Both must be approached in a state of love. Allow that dual mission to come from your spirit through your heart into your mind.

This means that you need to be honest with yourself, it means that you need to look inside at your own vulnerability and weakness - not at that of others - because if you understand your own vulnerability and weakness then you can only have respect for others. And what more could you possibly hope for than to see reflected in those around you what you know is inside you. This is what it is about, isn't it, your mission in this lifetime - to help to bring love, balance and understanding, moving the whole planet beyond the need of judgement and manipulation.

All the great masters have taught this, but when it comes to that personal part, humankind carefully avoids it and wants to lay blame: 'It is not my fault', they say, but whose fault is it? Fault can only happen if there is a reaction on two sides, it cannot happen in any other way. In one sense there is no such thing as fault, it is only how you see it, because fault is the result of your free will and choice. And, in my opinion, there is no such thing as right or wrong in this context, there is only what is.

God does not judge, why do you have to judge? God does not condemn, why do you need to condemn? God does not criticise, why do you need to criticise? God does not manipulate, why do you need to manipulate?

It is because of your own insecurity, because of your own lack of awareness of that true spiritual impulse inside. You are the person who judges yourself at the end of the day, no one else, and if there is such a thing as hell when you pass over, it is a state that you create for yourself.

So, look at your lives, dear friends, and say to yourself, 'How fortunate I am! Yes, I have been into my own hell and back, I haven't liked it, but I value it because it is helping me to see the love and beauty on this planet despite what has happened.'

Then there is the spirit, that part of you that has been through many experiences long before you came into the possibility of incarnating into *homo sapiens*. What wonderful spirits you all are! Each one of you represents the sum total of all that you have ever been, carrying the pleasure, carrying the hurt, carrying the liberation, carrying the imprisonment, carrying all the resolved and unresolved issues of past lives. Where were you in your past life and the one before that and before that, perhaps stretching right back to Atlantis? You are certainly a flavour of all those past lives.

So, when your spirit makes a decision and chooses a body to come into and experience through, it is not just saying, 'Hmm, I think I fancy that one.' It is saying, 'This is going to be a life that carries the possibility of furthering my evolution. I may come into this physical body full of love and full of happiness, recognising my shadow and my vulnerability. I may come into this body with a lot of bitterness, with a lot of resentment - look what they did to me in my past life, look what I did in my past life! I was a fiend, I was a coward; I was tortured, I was invaded, I was raped!'

All that is within each one of you. You may have been a leader of a country. You may have been the poorest, most downtrodden peasant. I believe that you can learn as much from being the lowliest, humblest, downtrodden peasant, as you can from being in charge of a country. For each carries a different message, you need to be both to understand the other - the ruler needs to understand the needs of the peasant, the peasant needs to understand the needs of the ruler.

This is where we are today, so many wise spirits incarnating, carrying that energy of the past, dealing with past beliefs that they have been unable to release and let go of, such as a belief that it is a sin even to consider reincarnation, for your spirit will be cursed if you do! Despite all these misconceptions, it is important to go on. Perhaps another spirit will try to help you, release you, lift you to where suddenly you begin to see the light and you begin to realise there is no such thing as a fixed belief. You begin to see that you can actually move beyond it and that all thought in the universe is infinite - as spirit we are infinite, we have no boundaries. The only boundaries are those which we create.

As pure spirit, although you have individuality and you are unique, you are a creation of the Godhead, and you are inexorably linked to that Godhead because you are part of it. You may even reach a point in your life when you reject the Godhead and say, 'I am my own God.' That is a very painful state to be in because you can only follow that route by controlling others, by not allowing others to consider that there is a God. Taken to an extreme, you could drive people into believing that the best way they can serve God is by killing themselves.

It is exhausting to think about and consider all the complexities, and yet it is exciting because, knowing that we are linked to the Godhead, we can allow our spirits to soar and reach up to that light and to realise that everything from a spiritual point of view is possible. A belief in God is not about following a deity; it is about acknowledging your self-worth. It is about feeling that God energy inside you - how it can empower you and empower others around you in an equal way.

9/11 and its effect

9/11 occurred because America was becoming increasingly balanced on top of a pin with nowhere to go; yet within that great country there is so much wisdom. There is also much blindness and it is about allowing the two to come together. That tragedy is only the first of many if they do not wake up to their responsibilities.

In conclusion, what happened on 9/11 and has been continued through the vagaries of nature is handing humanity the greatest opportunity that this planet has had for 2000 years. For many things are returning to be resolved, in order to really move things forward in a global way. I know there are those who oppose globalisation because they are fearful of individual power within it. What I can say to you is that if you wish to find the world peace that you seek, it is the only way forward; and when you accept that, then you can start to deal with having a balance within that concept.

So it is about loosening yourself from your ancestral roots. It is about saying, 'I am not only a Christian, I am also a Buddhist, a follower of Islam, a Jew, I understand the wisdom of Confucius and so on. What I have is my own individual approach and it is right for me. I can feel the God energy within me resonating'. Let it fill your heart, let it fill your lungs, let it fill your mind, let your spirit and mind come together and allow yourself to stand up and be counted! Speak your truth; speak from your heart but in love. Not in fear, in love. Not in condemnation, in love. Not in manipulation, just in love. Planetary Healing starts with you.

PEACE HEALING

You are indeed privileged to be incarnate at this great moment in Earth's evolution, at this meeting point between the past and the future. For this is the moment of a great shift in consciousness as the planet transits from one great Solar Age to the next. I consider Peace Healing to be one of the most significant healing concepts I have yet introduced because of what is happening on the planet at this very moment. Prevention is always better than cure.

This type of healing will not compel the receiver, but it will offer them the opportunity to look beyond the old Piscean Age strictures of 'right and wrong' and to realise that if there is such a thing as right and wrong, it exists within all people. On one level there is no such thing as right and wrong; but there is action and reaction. Forgiveness is about moving beyond the need to react, realising that the way forward is through listening and understanding, appreciating that everyone has a point of view even though it may differ from your own.

I see Peace Healing as a dedicated form of unconditional love, offering a unique opportunity to both the giver and the receiver. It can only be offered to them and they might reject it; they have the right to reject it. But the very nature of Peace Healing is that it will go to such a fine depth, to such a delicate frequency, that it will create movement inside one's being that other forms of healing will not touch. It can be sent either to a person in conflict, a couple, a group, an organisation or to a situation.

PEACE HEALING EXERCISE
Relax yourself and become conscious of your auric space strongly surrounding you, protecting you. Feel a sense of balance within, using the equidistant cross if you wish . . .

Now become aware of the energy around you getting lighter and finer and, as you reach to the God Source and begin to channel healing energy, see it divide to meet the light and the shadow within the receiver. . . So you are healing both the light and the shadow of that person or that spirit . . . It would be easier to use both hands in the process so that you can feel the energy coming from the palms of your two hands. Place them quite near the healee, whether they are present or distant.

Feel both the negative and the positive energies: the shadow and the light, the despair and the joy, the fear and the love, the rejection and the forgiveness . . . and lift those energies within your patient or patients, lift them right up above them . . . and then gently and slowly bring them together to form an additional chakra above the body, a spinning orb of chakric energy. I am going to call it the Peace Chakra. . . . Allow those opposing energies to spin round together . . . Then gently move your hands apart and allow that integrated energy to come right down through

116

the four levels of your patient: the spirit, the mind, the emotions and the body, at the same time feeling the link between those levels and that vortex of energy, the Peace Chakra.

Then, conforming to the cosmic law of three requests, three challenges, bring those energies together again in the Peace Chakra and down through the spirit, mind, emotions and body . . . And then a third time, so as to fulfil the karma of that healing. . . This time, connect the Peace Chakra with the crown chakra, which will then connect with the other six major chakras . . . this will create a feeling of liberation within your patient and that feeling of liberation will free them at a very deep spiritual level from their fear: the fear of doing the 'wrong' thing, the fear of having to do the 'right' thing. It will open them out to want to start to listen to what the other person or persons have to say.

Complete your healing in the usual way, strengthening the receiver's aura and returning in consciousness to your own body, aware of your own auric field. Centre and ground yourself. . . .

Now, it is not such a big step to contemplate that this form of healing can be extended to address difficult global situations, although it would be best undertaken by an experienced healing group. At this moment in time the world is moving towards yet another major confrontation and it is of paramount importance that all like-minded spirits who are incarnate now for the reason to serve humanity, should bond together to help the planet forward through this very unsettled time.

To send Peace Healing to a world leader in a trouble spot on Earth, or to a group of insurgents planning some atrocity, or to the management of a business unwilling to stop polluting the environment, requires a very strong resolve; but this kind of global healing is much needed.

There will be many innovative forms of healing started over the coming decades. Most of them will represent what the planet is ready for, ready to use and apply. This concept of Peace Healing is required to ease some of the pressing and difficult issues being faced on your planet today.

Chapter 13

SPECIAL TOPICS

A Spiritual Understanding of Cancer

Even spiritual seekers have difficulty in facing their shadow selves. They know that jealousy, hatred and resentment are attributes to be avoided, yet when these feelings are suppressed, this results in an imbalance which causes cells to mutate. It is important to understand what has caused a cancer to manifest before it can be dealt with.

A Global Experience
Cancer, as you know it, is a proliferation of mutating cells, which begins to affect the other cells in the body and then take them over. It affects the whole structure and balance of the psyche. This is why in the longer term the healing treatment of cancer can only come about through a body/mind/spirit approach. It is not simply a cause and effect; it is about the whole person, the whole being, the whole planet.

On your planet there is a proliferation of negative energies and cells; it is happening on every level of the planet. It is happening in your soil, it is happening in the animal kingdoms, the vegetable kingdoms, the mineral kingdoms; it doesn't actually help for humankind to develop new forms of mutation - sorry, you call it genetic engineering, I call it mutation. There is only one way for this planet to evolve and that is in a natural, open, organic way.

There are mutations taking place in your animal kingdoms, some of which have been inspired by man. The balance of energy in your soil is being affected, not only by humankind, but also through its own initiative. You must remember that all the kingdoms on your planet are complementary, they are each of equal importance to the planet, and whether they are animal, vegetable or mineral, they are going through a similar form of evolution as you are. In other words, it is physical substance being motivated by spirit.

As I have expressed earlier, your spirit came into your body at the moment of conception and chose your body for the kind of challenges that were going to be presented. There is no right or wrong in this, there is not even anything good or evil about it; it is only what you are and what you have been.

The important thing is the relationship between the various parts of you, the spirit, the soul, the subtle bodies, the chakras, the etheric body, the aura and the physical body. They are all part of the whole and it is necessary to find and maintain a balance between all these various aspects of your being; for, in addition, that balance can be affected by the overall polarity of energies in the universe.

Free will, Choice and Balance
One of the greatest gifts that each of you has is that of free will and choice; but it is also a gift that can lead you into some difficult, troubled waters. For unless you can face the fear in you, unless you can face the shadow in you, unless you can face the anger, resentment, jealousy and hatred within you – for that is all part of you - you will not find that balance. It is not that you are good or bad; it is that you are a composite being made up of every thought that you have ever made in any lifetime and in any state of experience in spirit.

Every spirit, to me, is beautiful; every spirit, to me, is wise; every spirit has the capacity to find love, even unconditional love that exists on the finest possible levels. But in the process of finding that love one also finds the vulnerability and the weaknesses. After all, if you were perfect you would not need to be in a physical body. If you had that perfect balance you would be of such divine beauty and such exquisite energy and love that you would be part of the Godhead itself. Where I speak from, beyond the physical, I no longer have the need to incarnate and can see from a wider perspective. But I am still light and shadow, I still have to face those aspects of my being. And the light and shadow that I face is far more exaggerated than that which you face because as I grow in wisdom and understanding, so my concepts of light and shadow become stronger and the challenge to find that sensitive balance between the two, greater.

In addition, on your planet you have the collective consciousness of the groups with which you have selected to incarnate. You have the collective consciousness of archetypes: of races, tribes, religions, beliefs and, in addition, you have the collective consciousness of the planet. And because the energy on and around your planet is becoming more and more intense, it is placing a greater emphasis, a greater need, a greater challenge for each one of you to find and maintain that level of balance within yourselves.

Cells mutate because there is a lack of balance. This is not a criticism or a judgment, it is an observation; because if you become out of balance between your spirit and all those levels of consciousness that make you up as a whole being, you will not vibrate in harmony, your auric field will be weakened and you will eventually attract some form of disease. And the form of disease that you will attract will be one which has an empathy with your emotional and spiritual state. It may also have an empathy with the type of life that you lead, the type of foods that you eat, the type of work that you do. For if you allow your being to become out of balance, mutations will take place and a certain kind of mutated cell will cause what you call cancer.

So, what is the best way that you can help yourself or help others who find that this is the form of disease that they have unconsciously attracted? Well, of course, you will need to consider why you think you have it. And it is really important to understand that it is not a sin to have cancer, it is not wrong to have it. It is a part of the corporate growth of the planet at this time and all the energies that are being brought to bear upon it, as it finally moves into the Age of Aquarius in 2012. Many things are going to happen between now and then, believe me, and that is why the amount of cancer on your planet is heavily on the increase and will continue to increase. The answer to it will not be through orthodox medicine alone. It will lie increasingly with the ability of the person to deal with themselves, to understand why they have drawn this energy to them that is creating a mutation of their cells. Sometimes it can be a deep cry for change on one level or another.

A wonderful opportunity

Cancer is a disease which somehow has created the wrong kind of publicity, carrying a kind of negative energy even just to talk about it. Whereas I would see it as a most wonderful challenge for the recipient, something to encourage them to say to themselves: "This is a moment for me to look at where and how I am, to evaluate my life. Why have I got into this state of imbalance? What can I do about it?" It is not just about destroying the mutated cells, it is about understanding why they are there and how you can grow beyond the need of them.

When dis-ease occurs – and, let us face it, in the construction and evolution of the human body as it is at the present time, imbalances are taking place and manifesting in different ways – any disease is reflecting something in the person, both emotionally and spiritually. Maybe there is hurt in this life or past lives - usually both - that has accumulated and reached a point within where on a very deep level such people feel that they are no longer able to cope. It may be that they want to find an answer, something that on one level they can even blame, something that is reflecting where they are and what is happening to their physical body, what is happening emotionally and spiritually within their physical body. What is the impasse?

Clearly, it is a time to sit back and reflect, a time to open up as far as you can, spiritually and emotionally, to understand what is going on at a deep level within you that has triggered that mutation reflected in your body.

The beginning of a new experience.

I regard cancer as one of the most interesting and, if I may say so, exciting challenges of your time. It is not the end of life; it is the beginning of a new experience. Deal with that experience, move beyond the need of it, and you can move into your next lifetime a free person, a free spirit unencumbered by the issues that have brought you to this state in your present life. If you don't face it, it could proliferate and bring up an uncontrolled and deep anger that will manifest in your next life, an energy that might want to mutate society, that might want to mutate the people with whom you live and associate.

So, it is actually a very important challenge – one that needs to be looked at, not with fear, but with love, gentleness, understanding, acceptance and joy. It is your Self saying to you,

"This is a moment in my life when I need to re-state who I am, what I am, where I am. This is a moment in my life when I need to live my truth, to say what I really feel, to say what I really mean - a time to cast aside some of those fears that I have found difficult to face and difficult to talk about in the past."

Past lives come into it because in the mission with which you have come into this life, you are bringing issues that will attract the type of conditions in which you find yourself.

For example, you may be attracted to a form of employment where you have to deal with substances that can give you cancer. That doesn't happen by accident; it is a big challenge for you to move beyond issues of blame, guilt and resentment - all those kinds of emotions that get triggered. Anyone who gets cancer must ask themselves 'Why me?' And I would like to suggest that 'Why me?' is a question that can be answered with confidence. It is because you have *chosen* this form of experience, for it is a form of experience that can uplift you, take you forward and help you release what has been ground down and stuck inside you. And as I said earlier, I see cancer as not exclusive to the human race; it is reflecting the whole state of your planet at this moment in time.

A more responsible approach to procreation
It also brings up an issue that I wish to speak about very sensitively. When a man and a woman come together to procreate they are taking on a very big responsibility for they are allowing a spirit to come into incarnation. Good, yes. But they are also affecting the population of the planet, the resources and needs of the planet, and the balance between *homo sapiens* and other forms of evolution on the planet - the animal kingdoms, the fish kingdoms, the bird kingdoms, the vegetable kingdoms and so on.

The act of procreation – as distinct from the sexual act - was not meant to be done in an indiscriminate and irrational way. And one of the big challenges that humankind will have to face in this coming age is: how many children do we have, what is the sex act all about, what is love and how can we bring all these issues together? It is not only a man's or a woman's individual decision, it is something that has to be decided within a group energy and group guidance. It is an area where spiritual teachings and religions need to start to under-stand what is happening on the planet and how they can affect the future.

In one sense, the way in which the human race is proliferating is a cancer in itself. Pretty heavy symbolism, is it not? That is not meant as a criticism or judgment on any belief system, because each has evolved to where it is now based on past life experience and understanding. But we are now moving into another age in which the challenges are very different and it is really important that those involved in spiritual teachings teach in such a way that enables people to take responsibility for the number of children they produce. Whilst I admire and express my heartfelt gratitude to all those wonderful people who raise money to send food to the starving millions, it is a situation that needs to be looked at on a much deeper level.

Those are my thoughts, dear friends, on the symbolic significance of cancer on your planet. Yes, I believe cancer can be dealt with; but, in the longer term, it must be dealt with as a whole, on a body/mind/spirit basis. If every cancer patient can be helped to understand their responsibility in having this disease and the wonderful opportunity it presents for them to look at their lives, they will see how, through helping themselves, they can give out unconditional love and help to their fellow beings around them.

My message is not one of gloom and doom, it is one of hope and opportunity; and I feel that looked at in the right way, it can help carry this planet forward safely into the Age of Aquarius. I have made some fairly strong statements, but they are made with love and without judgment. They are made in the hope that the human heart within the human body can communicate with the human spirit to bring forward a more loving way into the future.

Hereditary tendencies

Certainly cell mutations can run in families but a much more important issue is: 'What has your spirit chosen in this lifetime and what makes your heart sing?' Are you able to think through your heart? Are you able to express yourself though your heart? Very often labels are given and they can be very confusing. One that I hear being expressed time and time again is: 'smoking causes cancer.' Does it? Should not everyone who smokes have cancer in that case? They do not. What is it within a person that creates the need to smoke, heightening the dangers of the disease? I would be much more interested to find out what is within that person's soul memory that creates the compulsion to smoke as being the only way of dealing with a problem.

Simply because your parents had a particular disease does not mean that you will necessarily follow in their footsteps. On the other hand, you chose a body that was a product of your parents, so it will obviously bring forward some of their needs, some of their fears. Some of what they are is going to mingle with what you are and what you are seeking and wishing to find.

Allow that wisdom to rise up within you so that you can say to yourself, "How can I help others by what I am, what I believe in and what I do? How can my experience help them forward and help me forward at the same time?" I see in you a creative side that is very important for you to express. So, if it is possible for you to grow out instead of growing in, I think you will find it rewarding to start to honour yourself, to value yourself and to respect yourself for all those wonderful, unexpressed qualities that are part of you as a whole being. Allow yourself to stand up and be counted. The following is a HEALING MEDITATION. . .

Take a deep breath, breathe in the divine energy that surrounds you . . . feel it touching your spirit . . . feel it making your whole body want to expand in the most beautiful, loving way. . . There is so much love in your heart, allow it to expand, allow it to grow outwards. . . Each of you has so much to give in your life. Ask yourself how you would like to be able to give it. Can you feel it? Can you feel that stirring within? . . .

You are each unique, as is every spirit on the planet. Value that uniqueness. Respect it, honour it, feel the love, allow me and my colleagues to come to you, allow us to touch your spirit, to encourage it to express what it can express and what it will express with your motivation behind it. . . . You each need to acknowledge the joy, the expansiveness and the creativity within you and find ways of expressing it. . . .

Feel the energy (individually or as a group) going round in a clockwise direction, spiralling right up though the roof, reaching out with unconditional love to all parts of the planet. . . . Allow that unconditional love to touch the hearts of those who carry anger and those who want revenge and retribution. Help them to understand that God is a God of love, unconditional love that means total forgiveness, and feel those qualities within yourself as you gently return to your body . . . .

Re-earth yourself, centring and re-aligning yourself within your physical body. . . My blessings to each and every one of you.

The Spiritual Effects of Drug-taking

Impatience and escapism are rife in your developed world today. Everyone wants the quick fix and the instant cure. Many spiritual seekers demand the ultimate experience without having to work for it. We will look at how damaging this is to the soul

To begin, we need to decide what we mean by a drug. From my perspective, it is any substance which interferes with the balance of the different 'levels of being' in your body: the chakras, the subtle bodies, the aura and the physical body; and which destroys the ability of the native spirit to be in control.

When I talk about the effects of drug taking, I am talking about not only those that are used for entertainment, for escape, for release, but also those that are administered by doctors, because they equally can affect the stability of the balance within. And I find this very fascinating because so often you'll hear orthodox medicine saying, "This is the right drug for this condition" and then further tests show that it isn't right for that person at this time, for they are not taking into account the stability, resonance and balance of the spirit inside the body.

So, it depends on the individual and what each has been subjected to. It is also about dealing with the psychological aspects underlying the condition, the fear and doubts, and nearly everybody has those fears and doubts. In other words, "Am I good enough to contact my Higher Self? What have I been? What happens if I'm out of control?" As you start to go through your life and experience, there is that inner part of you that is trying to contact what you have been. You may shut it out totally saying, "I don't believe in all that stuff." You may want to use it to repay what has happened in a past life so you come in with a lot of anger wanting to kill or harm, or maybe sacrifice yourself because you feel this is the right thing to do.

This shows you how important it is to really come to terms with that inner part of you, accepting that you are both right and wrong, accepting that you are both light and shadow, but also accepting that you can bring these two sides to blend together and find a harmony.

The pressures and demands of their tribal culture place tremendous stresses on people, leading to a lack of understanding in families, abuse by parents towards their children, mental, physical, sexual, all these forms of abuse. So, somewhere along the line the group consciousness reacts to this. It is the group consciousness which arose after the last world war when there was so much frustration, so much unhappiness, bitterness and anger that the spirit started to look for other ways of relieving stress.

The Consequences

Alcohol is one way, but drugs offer a different form of release because they affect you on a deeper level, and I'm talking about hallucinatory drugs, the type of thing that people buy on street corners. These not only loosen the contact between the spirit and the body, but they remove levels of ability for the person to understand and so behave in a sensible way. It is really creating a divide between the spirit and the physical body that goes very deep, but in it they find a release that enables the spirit to leave the body and look down.

Because of the circumstances under which the drugs have been taken, the spirit will be looking for things that exaggerate, that blow you open still further. And when you are out of the body in that drugged state you will find yourself beginning to attract other such spirits, negative energies, all kinds of causes and symptoms that will blow your life apart. Now the answer to this is not in advice or counselling. The only long term answer is in the consciousness of the collective shifting onto another dimension where it can move beyond the need for this form of what is called 'relaxation'. For I see this as a state of total panic, in which a person is living in an aura of make-believe, travelling around on the astral seeing wherever their spirit takes them.

This can also happen with any medical drug that breaks the link between the spirit, the mind and the body. So you may take a drug from your doctor for a particular dis-ease with the best of feeling; but in dealing with that condition the drug can easily break down other lines of immunity and defence within the body's systems. In many cases, where a medical drug is concerned, the side effects can be far more dangerous spiritually than any form of addiction. In that respect it is worse than alcohol.

The long-term consequences

I intend now to discuss the serious consequences of drug-taking for so-called uplifting purposes, which includes cases of people who take drugs to help them over some difficult situation, as well as those who do so in the hope of gaining some form of psychic or so-called spiritual experience, as the effect is more or less the same.

This is the Aquarian Age, the age of the mind, and man is trying to seek into his mind and penetrate the depths of that strange computer-like object he calls the brain. This is not new for he has been engaged in such studies for many years, but he is constantly seeking new techniques to aid him in his quest. Perhaps he is looking for short cuts as well? There are those who suffer under the very false delusion that the taking of drugs is a short cut. On the surface it may appear to be so, but a short cut to what - to escape? As I see it, it is a short cut to the complete breakdown of integration within the person and to the complete and wanton destruction of the physical vehicle. So what is then left? The whole purpose for spirit incarnating into physical life is lost. To put it in a nutshell, drug-taking is the surest and quickest way of retarding the evolution of the individual.

Am I being too harsh? Am I failing to go with the trend? Any spirit that comes to a planet to throw some form of light into the darkness has to try to keep things moving, for stagnation is retrogression. We cannot therefore condone any form of negative teaching, because negation does not help anybody. If you individually are interested in developing yourselves psychically and spiritually, you must go forward positively with clear-cut thinking. Your first objective should be to ascertain your goal and, with many people, this may take many years or even many lives!

What happens when you take a drug?
The control between the spirit and the physical brain is affected according to the type and potency of the drug and which parts of the subconscious are released. Many of you must be familiar with the results of an excessive intake of alcohol when portions of your conscious control are relinquished, with sometimes amusing but more often pathetic results. From a psychic point of view, certain drugs induce similar processes, but the difference between drugs and alcohol lies in the speed of effect on the metabolism of the body. The drug strikes deeper, the lack of control is increased and the spirit immediately leaves the body and enters the astral planes.

If a person is trying to achieve a subliminal experience, and he takes a drug in anticipation of achieving such an end, his own power of thought will aid the process in the earlier stage. I cannot emphasise to you sufficiently the effects of the power of thought. When a person dies and the spirit leaves the body, that which is left of the essence of that particular personality lives on in a state of thought. Consequently, the state of mind prevailing at the time of passing is important to further spiritual evolution.

Now, when an incarnate spirit leaves the body as a result of drug-taking, it is projected onto a thought plane; the connection between the subconscious and the conscious mind is loosened and, consequently, any experiences undergone on the spirit plane are easily relayed upon return to the body. Thus a form of psychic experience is effected. But, unfortunately, the drug is having a deteriorating effect on the body so that the actual mechanism of the brain is becoming slowly enfeebled. Perhaps the first few sessions will prove quite agreeable but, remember, the spirit is being catapulted onto a plane upon which it has no proper form of control. There is no one there to watch over it and see that it does not come to any harm. By its own actions it has rejected its spirit helpers.

This form of ejection of the spirit from the body is completely unnatural. It causes bewilderment to the spirit because there is still the link to the body while the psychic consciousness is operating on a false freedom. If the person becomes addicted to the drug and then has to increase the dose, the physical body begins to degenerate. Those who have become complete addicts will know within themselves the form of suffering which is undergone, although to a person who is not a drug-taker this is almost imposs-ible to understand. Perhaps the most terrifying aspect of this is the form of revulsion which addicts feel within themselves for what they have done and are doing.

It seems strange that, although many drug addicts profess love and non-violence, they are unable to extend this philosophy to the preservation and welfare of their own physical vehicle, the components of which have as much right to consideration as the principles the addict preaches.

Anti-experience

Let us look for a moment at the question of anti-experience. You know that the spirit experiences physically through a process of reincarnation. It chooses its body for each life and enters it at the moment of conception with the knowledge that that particular life could offer a certain type of karma that it needs. This experience begins at the moment the spirit joins the embryo. The challenge of your life is to carry out that chosen karma within the realms of those cosmic laws which govern physical experience. However, there are certain forms of experience which are entirely alien to the physical body which I would call anti-experience, and these include the alienation of the mind from normal physical living, that is, when the mind does not accept the body and tries to live constantly in the world of the spirit.

I can assure you that no one experiences the higher planes through any artificial or unnatural means such as drug-taking. Contrary to what they may believe, drug-takers do not take a trip to these higher realms; their experiences are usually undergone on the astral planes that can afford a spirit a very wide range of experience, varying from colourful impressions to the horrific nightmares of a 'bad trip'.

In order to experience on the higher planes it is necessary to ascend through a series of natural psychic and spiritual develop-ments called initiations. Spirits can only attain to such exalted realms when they are ready to go there. It is a process of evolution, of gaining wisdom, and there are no short cuts to spiritual evolution. To unlock the door you must first acquire the wisdom to turn the key and you cannot acquire such wisdom from the contents of a bottle! Wisdom is attained over many incarnations through the resolution of karma. And karma is something from which you cannot escape. You cannot avoid it, you cannot cheat it.

Is Healing Possible?

Unfortunately, from an esoteric point of view, it is extremely difficult to help a person who is under the influence of a drug, for the healer is faced with half a person, in effect. Healing, to be effective, must be absorbed by the spirit which then relays it to the physical body. If the spirit is continually being forced away from the body, it cannot relay that healing power that could have brought it into a state of wholeness.

The 'I', the soul, the ego, that spark which motivates your body, enters at the moment of conception in order to undergo forms of physical experience. Its controlling mechanism is very sensitive and the liaison or link which connects it with its physical shell is in a delicate balance, to say the least, so that it does not require much to destroy this equilibrium. Most of you have some slight imbalance between the spirit and the body, for as beings incarnate on a physical plane you are not perfect; but it is only when these imbalances become accentuated that serious problems set in. One factor which can affect the balance is modern day living with its noise, tension and false pace of life. Imbalances in the human body bring about some form of illness, and this is, in effect, a mutation in itself. Not only is there the possibility of cancer but also of degenerative diseases such as Parkinson's.

So, to return to leisure drugs - what can we do about them? If you find or you know of somebody who has this problem, of course you could help them by counselling them to understand why they have the need to take the drug. Because once that can become a total reality, then they can move gently into exploring ways of moving beyond the need of it.

The Natural Procedures

Interestingly, I think the emphasis now taking place in complementary medicine is very important, because so many of the techniques used are about creating balance, understanding the cause; they are not about destroying something. You see, this is one of the big differences. Most orthodox western medicine is about dealing with a symptom. Healing techniques are about bringing together, creating harmony and balance and enabling that person to find a new way forward. So whether it is acupuncture, chiropractic, osteopathy, nutrition, energy healing or one of the new therapies that are coming up, whatever system is being used, they all play a part in bringing a balance back into that person's life. They can often work alongside medical drugs and many complementary therapies can be of considerable significance in dealing with drug abuse.

One of the forms of complementary medicine that I would place very highly in this respect is energy healing which can penetrate down to a similar depth that the drug has and it will ease it, move it and surface it. It is because this drug has gone so deep into a person's psyche that, when they are 'off' it, they are still aware of it being there and it makes them come back to it again and again and again. So, if you are giving healing to a client with this problem, make sure that the energy you are using is going to the very deepest level to help create a balance.

The other aspect that healing energy and other therapies such as psychotherapy, counselling and hypnotherapy will encompass, is to help deal with any negative energy that the person's drug problem has attracted towards them. That negative energy may be a lost spirit, because if your spirit is 'lost' in you, it is going to attract other lost spirits; and there are millions of lost spirits over the centuries who have been forced out of their bodies in a violent way through torture, murder, in cataclysms etc. They are still lost and don't know which way to turn, and when they see another lost spirit their reaction is, "Oh that's wonderful, I can team up with it!" For that lost spirit in the human body is carrying a different energy from that of a balanced person and this will attract another lost spirit.

This for me is one of the big problems for people who are taking drugs. They draw this negative energy towards themselves which

131

creates more shadow and brings out their destructive side. And often that will be self-destructive as well as wanting to hurt or destroy others.

Passing on

When the physical body can take no more, the spirit finally moves on. It leaves that body knowing, usually, that the drug has prevented it from discharging its karma in that life, for drug-taking is not a natural form of experience and could even be described, as I said earlier, as a form of anti-experience. You see, that person has systematically destroyed his or her own body by deliberately breaking the elemental patterns of which it was composed.

When a person dies by taking too many drugs, an overdose, that spirit will leave the body in a very confused and lost state and when it looks back on its life and evaluates what it did, it's going to feel very sad, very sorry for itself, and maybe very angry with itself and possibly with others. Often a spirit in that state will seize the opportunity to attach itself to a living person who has a similar addiction. And it may take some time before it reincarnates because it is in a state of total confusion and will not be ready to listen to anybody, spirit or otherwise.

Beyond death

From this you can see that a person who destroys himself through drug-taking has usually avoided the karma for which he has entered that body, because he has spent portions of that life going through forms of anti-experience. To make matters worse, he has abandoned his body for long periods before actual death because the spirit has been forcibly ejected by the action of the drug.

Sometimes, while the addict is on a 'trip', the body becomes temporarily possessed by another spirit. This is a most unpleasant experience as the possessing spirit is unable to control the body while it is under the effects of the drug and this can result in a fit of uncontrollable violence which the person cannot account for once the effect of the drug has worn off.

All the time, then, there is this programme of destruction and the native spirit is left in a state of complete humiliation, degeneration and bewilderment. Unfortunately, it usually takes a long time before that spirit can work through the karmic barriers it has erected about itself. Past life therapy might well be helpful in this situation. There is no penitence worse than self-inflicted penitence; there is no torture worse than the torture of a spirit that has completely frustrated itself.

Once such a spirit leaves its body there is the additional frustration that it can no longer rely upon the drug to ferry it into a series of astral experiences. Without artificial aids it is reliant upon its own power of thought which it has not been in the habit of using. So, the experiences it has enjoyed are denied it for, without a body, they cannot be bought by a 'fix'. Such is the torture of the addict whose supply has been permanently cut off.

I was pleased that this lecture was titled the spiritual aspects of drug-taking because it undoubtedly affects a person's own spiritual evolution. Remember, God loves you all. God offers you unconditional love, forgiveness and respect. Hear that! Feel it! Experience it in every part of your being because that love is the one thing that the shadow cannot deal with. The stronger your love, the stronger will be your respect for what you are, how you are and who you are, without ego, without pretending to be what you are not. Yet, at the same time you are evaluating yourself, seeing yourself, understanding yourself and being yourself. These are all important factors.

Remaining True to Yourself

The trap of spiritual pride

I would like now to go beyond the realms of drug-taking and touch on some other pitfalls which are just as dangerous. In the eastern world, forms of meditation have developed over a number of years and many of them have been designed for the upliftment of the soul. Some of these have penetrated westwards but, like most things which come from the East to the West, they have been adapted to meet the way of the westerner. It is important to realise that in the East there is an entirely different approach to spiritual thinking - inherited and developed through the centuries - from the approach which has evolved in western civilization.

Certain forms of meditation used in the East can be, in my opinion, extremely dangerous to the westerner, especially if they involve the relinquishing of mental control. The westerner should always try to think positively but never beyond that of which he is capable. Unfortunately, there are types of meditation at the present time which have come from the East which tempt man to step beyond the realms of his own capabilities; they encourage meditation of a passive nature which can ultimately produce a similar effect, from the psychic point of view, as drug-taking.

I view all forms of receptive meditation without protection as dangerous because those who seek this type of short cut to spiritual experience rarely understand what is happening to them; and if they should fall into the category of those who think they do know the answers they are even more dangerous.

I shall enlarge upon this a little more because meditation is a subject about which I feel very strongly. I see it as a practise which should be carried out only under strict supervision or within a disciplined framework or protection. It is a simple psychological trick to use a form of pseudo-positive meditation and enforce people to over-concentrate on one idea in order to make the mind susceptible. This technique has, in fact, the effect of creating a vacuum in the mind, which in itself can be very dangerous. I do not wish to enter into too much detail on this as it is very much an esoteric matter and I am trying to point a moral rather than give a list of 'dos' and 'don'ts'.

The moral is a simple one. In any form of seeking man must guard himself against his own personal vanity. It is very easy in the beginning to say, "I am going to have a go at this, because I can always pull myself out at the last moment", or "I am going to have that or do this, because I know I can always stop." I am quite sure that most addicts have said this at some time or other.

The same type of vanity unfortunately prevails amongst many spiritual seekers. They see in their astral experiences a form of entertainment or escape which exists purely for their amusement; they convince themselves that it is furthering their spiritual evolution and they blindly claim immunity from any detrimental consequences. Man must learn never to push himself beyond that which he knows in his true Self he is capable of achieving. If he follows this principle he cannot go wrong. *Remember, that the moment of finding your importance is the moment of losing it.*

At the same time he must think and work positively and progressively within this framework; for this in itself is a step on the ladder of evolution. As I have always taught, the plan of the world is evolution, with the Godhead as the Ultimate.

Miracles

For me, there is only one form of miracle and that is when the spirit comes into harmonious alignment with the physical body, when there is a clarity of understanding, when there is a feeling of complete peace and acceptance of that inner part of your being. It is certainly not something dramatic, something you may see in a circus or even in a musical hall or on TV, it is not about the sudden and unexpected. It is the result of inner attunement. So dear friends, allow that miracle to happen as you read what I have said.

God

Who is God? What is God? How is God? We are all God. That Ultimate Energy is in every soul, it is in every cell of your physical body. It is about discovering and totally understanding that you are part of God, not just created by God. You are part of God and God is part of you. You are part of the experience of being God, of finding God, of allowing it to permeate, to percolate every aspect of your consciousness. And as that synchronicity begins to occur within you, that is a miracle. We are entering a period and a time of miracles when they are going to happen more and more.

So I say to you all that when you are thinking seriously and deeply, it is important that you allow yourself to move beyond judgement, even about people and spirits that you feel are trying to destroy the planet, whether through violence or through neglect. In some way those people are part of your shadow, they are part of the collective shadow and are reflecting that shadow. And if you are angry with them and reject them, you are feeding them; they need love - unconditional love - because that is what they are denying others. They are frightened to look inside and see that God energy within, because God energy is the very opposite to a boosted ego. It is about a gentle energy that reaches within as opposed to without.

So, when you hear expressions of grief for and loss of those who have been affected by some catastrophe, honour them, acknowledge them and try to enable them to see it in perspective. What was this saying? What is this saying? What are the opportunities that have been created? Those opportunities, my friends, are miracles, they are miracles in a sense that they are enabling people to look within in a way they have not looked within before, to question what the planet is and what it is trying to achieve. Is it on a course of destruction? Is it on a course of moving beyond destruction? Is it neither? No, dear friends, it is both.

This is all about humankind, the animal kingdoms, the mineral kingdoms, every expression of experience on your planet taking a new look, a deeper look within. Think about it. When you breathe, you feel the energy moving through your whole body. In that act of breathing is an act of spiritual unfoldment and wonder.

It is now more important than ever before for you, on an individual and collective basis, to allow that God energy within to speak forth; not to proclaim, not to judge, not to condemn, not to say you are right and every one else is wrong. Understand that for every right there is a wrong and for every wrong there is a right. Where is your right? Where is your wrong? Where is your wholeness? Where is that symbiosis within? It is not just about breathing in the light and breathing out the shadow, it is about breathing in both the light and the shadow, because that shadow not only represents the fear, it also represents the vulnerability and you need to be aware of both.

When beings on your planet talk about weapons of mass destruction, they are not talking about weapons, they are talking about individuals and the will and intent of individuals. People on this planet need to learn to listen, they need to learn to hear, to understand that there is another side to every question and every answer.

These people you call terrorists, are they villains? Are they instruments of evil? Of course not, they are expressing something in a way that is bursting forth because they feel unheard, they feel rejected. When you feel unheard and rejected, you want to express yourself, you want to do something to draw attention. And the ultimate way of doing that is through some act of suicide that embodies all that you believe. It is not new, it has happened for

136

thousands of years; it happened in your last war and it happened before and before and before.

The world will never sort itself out through force, through brutality, through murder and torture. Miracles happen when you can acknowledge that. Miracles happen when something inside you decides that it is ready to move forward, to take a fresh look at the universe, to take a fresh look at everything that you believe and do not believe. Wisdom is moving beyond belief, because belief implies unbelief, so you are once again in a polarising state. And yet, it is not a state of indecision, it is a state of total decision where one has found a moment or place of peace within.

FINAL MOMENT OF PEACE

When you allow yourself to open up to these thoughts and impulses, there is often a considerable change of energy. When that is so, I would ask you to sense it, to allow it, to enable it to reach through your heart to the source of your being. I invite you to join me in the following affirmation and say to yourself,

"In humility I acknowledge that I am part of the God energy and in that acknowledgement I honour my readiness to open my heart . . . to open my mind . . . to open my whole Self to the mission, to the reason why I have chosen this life. . . I honour my body, I honour my spirit, and I honour my whole being. . . I allow my being to open itself up to the energies of the Age of Aquarius. And that, in itself, will resonate with my choice of incarnation, with my own personal need to be what I can be in the unfoldment of the planet's journey forward.

I want to work to help save the planet, to help solve the problems on the planet, to help bring the planet into a new age of thinking and exploration - a new dimension of being. I feel this energy moving to and fro through my heart, touching my soul, touching my source of wisdom, bringing me into that state of being that is in itself a miracle . . . a miracle that will allow me to help my fellow beings, to help all the forms of evolution that make up planet Earth, that I may discover a gentleness in myself that I never knew I had before . . .

Let me help rescue the idea of God from the many egotistical, fearful concepts that have been placed on that Ultimate Energy.

Yes, of course God is here to help, but only if I ask for it in a way that embodies the whole principle of unconditional love, unconditional thinking, unconditional assessment of what I am."

So, dear friends, I challenge you to find that miracle within and allow it to manifest. Can you feel it? Can you sense it? Let us in our minds hold each other's hands, let us hold each other's hearts, and let us hold each other's spirits. May that energy of unconditional love, forgiveness and respect, enable you to say from the depths, from the source of your being,

"I am what I am, no more, no less. . . And in that statement is the very essence of my being, where I am on my spiritual journey and what I am learning and experiencing in this lifetime. May it help me always to hold within myself a little of the miracle of this moment.

"Let me take this miracle out into the world and spread it, offer it, and enable it to be sampled and touched. I am part of my own miracle and I offer that miracle to my fellow beings, to the animal kingdoms, to the plant kingdoms, to the mineral kingdoms, to all expressions of God's love, God's energy, that are necessary to bring wholeness to this planet Earth – planet of music, planet of sound, planet of healing. . . Allowing that resonance to take place within me enables me to give it forth."

That, dear friends, is what miracles are about. They are not trying to prove anything, they are about 'being'. It is a personal experience, not intended to be a demonstration of anything to anyone else but yourself, as an acknowledgement of the God energy of which you are part, which you can savour and offer and taste and experience and just 'be'.

In conclusion

I would like to emphasise again that as we move through this time of final preparation for the Age of Aquarius, which will reach its climax in 2012, there are waves of heightened energy sweeping into your atmosphere of Earth, permeating into the soul of your country, and into the waiting populace. More and more challenges are going to present themselves, more and more opportunities are going to arise, and some of these will need great skill to resolve.

Some conflicts will escalate still further before a resolution can be achieved. Alas, the types of emotional response that whip up communities to act harshly on their neighbours can only create more anger, more resentment and more hatred; because the strong influx of light at this time, which will continue until at least 2016, is touching something profound in each one of you, stirring up that light and shadow within every heart on the planet. Some will choose to ignore it because they are too frightened to even consider the implications. For it threatens the very structure of their understanding, of how to deal with what they regard as evil. Remember, the one thing that fear/shadow cannot deal with is love; it cannot deal with unconditional love.

At this time, when more and more people are becoming aware of being psychic, it is even more important for you to acknowledge the intuitional side of your being, to honour it, and to find out the way in which you want to express it. You can express it creatively in the things that you do in your life. You may do it with a combination of both the yin and the yang energies and become a healer/ medium, for the intuition activates the imagination in a very subtle way. Above all, you can use it to listen to and heed the words and impulses of the great spirit working through you into your life.

So, dear friends, feel that golden sphere of love energy in the centre of your room, feel it embracing and surrounding you. Allow yourself to respond to the higher energies, the finer energies of the universe and . . .

KNOW THAT YOU ARE TRULY LOVED.

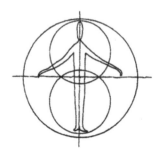

Some useful contacts:

College of Healing   Phone & Fax: 01295 26141
PO Box 568   Collegeofhealing@aol.com
Banbury
Oxon, OX16 6AW   www.collegeofhealing.org

Helios School of Healing   Phone & Fax 0207 7137125
116 Judd Street,   heliosc@dialstart.net
London WC1H 9NS   www.helioshealth.org.uk

School of Channelling   Phone: 01684 311345
PO Box 109   info@schoolofchannelling.co.uk
Worcester WR9 0ZY   www.schoolofchannelling.co.uk

Spirit Release Foundation
Frida Siton   Phone: 01684 560725
Myrtles   fridamaria@spiritrelease.com
Como Road
Malvern, WR14 3TH   www.spiritrelease.com

OTHER PUBLICATIONS BY 'THE EYE OF GAZA PRESS'

The Spirit Within
    Chan, through the mediumship of Ivy Northage

The Guide Book
    H-A, through the mediumship of Tony Neate

Gifts of the Spirit: Trance Channelling
    through mediums, Maisie Besant & Greg Branson

Akhenaten Speaks: The Nature of Spiritual Healing
    through the trance mediumship of Maisie Besant